Lessons Learned from Novice Teachers

Lessons Learned from Novice Teachers

An International Perspective

By

Kari Smith, Marit Ulvik and Ingrid Helleve

BRILL
SENSE

LEIDEN | BOSTON

All chapters in this book have undergone peer review.

The Library of Congress Cataloging-in-Publication Data is available online at http://catalog.loc.gov

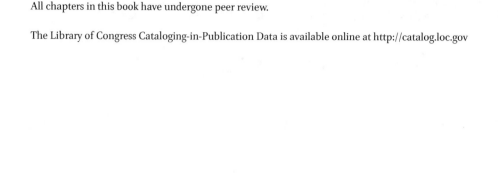

Typeface for the Latin, Greek, and Cyrillic scripts: "Brill". See and download: brill.com/brill-typeface.

ISBN 978-90-04-41308-5 (paperback)
ISBN 978-90-04-41309-2 (hardback)
ISBN 978-90-04-41310-8 (e-book)

Copyright 2019 by Koninklijke Brill NV, Leiden, The Netherlands.
Koninklijke Brill NV incorporates the imprints Brill, Brill Hes & De Graaf, Brill Nijhoff, Brill Rodopi, Brill Sense, Hotei Publishing, mentis Verlag, Verlag Ferdinand Schöningh and Wilhelm Fink Verlag.
All rights reserved. No part of this publication may be reproduced, translated, stored in a retrieval system, or transmitted in any form or by any means, electronic, mechanical, photocopying, recording or otherwise without prior written permission from the publisher.
Authorization to photocopy items for internal or personal use is granted by Koninklijke Brill NV provided that the appropriate fees are paid directly to The Copyright Clearance Center, 222 Rosewood Drive, Suite 910, Danvers, MA 01923, USA. Fees are subject to change.

This book is printed on acid-free paper and produced in a sustainable manner.

Contents

1 Learning to Swim without a Swim Belt: The First Year of Teaching   1
   1 Introduction   1
   2 Why Narratives?   2
   3 First Year of Teaching: A Year of Learning   3
   4 Mentoring and Collegial Support   4
   5 Main Challenges in the First Year of Teaching   5
   6 Resilience   6
   7 Conclusion   7

PART 1
The Australian Teacher Education Context

Introduction to Part 1: The Australian Context   13
John Loughran
   1 Structure of Teacher Education   13
   2 Status of Teaching Profession   13
   3 Employment   14

2 Carol's Story: Teaching Is Too Much Fun to Be a Real Job!   16
   1 Why Teacher?   16
   2 The Beginning   17
   3 To Become a Real Teacher   17
   4 High Expectations for the Future   19
   5 What Can We Learn from Carol's Story?   20
   6 Conclusion   22

3 Eric's Story: I Love the Spontaneity of My Profession   24
   1 Why Teacher?   24
   2 The Community of Learners   24
   3 The Beginning   25
   4 The Teacher as an Artist   26
   5 Demands from the Authorities   26
   6 The Community   27
   7 I Did What I Felt Was Correct   27
   8 Future Expectations   28
   9 What Can We Learn from Eric's Story?   30
  10 Conclusion   32

PART 2
The English Teacher Education Context

Introduction to Part 2: The English Context   37
Jean Murray

4 **Anna's Story: I Want to Share My Love of Languages**   39
    1   Motivation   39
    2   The Pastoral Care   39
    3   Characteristics of the School   40
    4   Support   40
    5   Ups and Downs   41
    6   What Does Anna's Story Tell?   42
    7   Conclusion   46

5 **Owen's Story: Empowering Students**   48
    1   My Job   48
    2   Likes, Dislikes and Aims   49
    3   The Support   50
    4   My Learning Outcome and Future   51
    5   What Does Owen's Story Tell?   52
    6   Conclusion   56

PART 3
The Finnish Teacher Education Context

Introduction to Part 3: The Finnish Context   61
Sven-Erik Hansén

6 **Alice's Story: I Cannot Save Everybody**   64
    1   The First Semester   64
    2   The Second Semester   65
    3   The Third Semester   65
    4   Support   66
    5   The Fourth Semester   66
    6   What Can We Learn from Alice's Story?   67
    7   Conclusion   69

7 **Maria's Story: I Have to Practice What I Preach**   71
    1   The Ethical Challenge   71
    2   Support   72

   3 The Autonomous Teacher   73
   4 Outside the Classroom   73
   5 What Can We Learn from Maria's Story?   74
   6 Conclusion   76

PART 4
The Israeli Teacher Education Context

Introduction to Part 4: The Israeli Context   81
   Lily Orland-Barak

8 Aviva's Story: Teaching Is a Call   84
   1 Becoming a Teacher   84
   2 Challenges and Rewards   84
   3 Critical Incidents   85
   4 Support   86
   5 Future Plans   87
   6 What Does Aviva's Story Tell Us?   87
   7 Conclusion   90

9 Yael's Story: Mary Poppins of Geography   92
   1 Motivation   92
   2 Challenges and Rewards   92
   3 Critical Incidents   93
   4 Support   94
   5 Looking Back   94
   6 What Does Yael's Story Tell Us?   95
   7 Conclusion   97

PART 5
The Norwegian Teacher Education Context

Introduction to Part 5: The Norwegian Context   101
   Marit Ulvik

10 Endre's Story: You Have to Try out Different Things   103
   1 My Classes   103
   2 Ups and Downs   105
   3 Support   106
   4 From Student to Teacher   107

	5	The Future 107
	6	What Does Endre's Story Tell? 108
	7	Conclusion 113

11 Eva's Story: Critical Thinking, a challenge and an Opportunity 116
    1 Becoming a Teacher 116
    2 Collaboration or Sharing 116
    3 Likes and Dislikes 117
    4 Critical Incidents 117
    5 What Does Eva's Story Tell? 118
    6 Conclusion 124

PART 6
Conclusions

12 Lessons Learned from the Teachers' Stories 129
    1 Introduction 129
    2 Motivation 130
    3 Expectations and Reality 132
    4 On-Job Learning 133
    5 Relations 135
    6 Mentoring/Support 137
    7 The Future 139
    8 Discussion 141
    9 Expectations and Reality 144
    10 Relations 146
    11 Lessons Learned 150

CHAPTER 1

Learning to Swim without a Swim Belt: The First Year of Teaching

1   Introduction

Most newly educated teachers experience challenges in their first year of teaching. We, the three authors of this book, remember well the difficulties we had to cope with in the first year of teaching, yet we stayed in the profession for a couple of decades before moving into teacher education and research. Interestingly enough, the challenges as first year teachers were rather similar, even though we were induced into the profession in three different contexts. We came from different backgrounds, and we graduated from rather different teacher education programmes. Marit tells about how terrible it was when she in her first job had to practice out of field teaching and taught music in four different classes, whereas Ingrid says that until a critical incident saved her in the middle of the first autumn, she really wanted to drop out. Kari learnt a lot about how not to handle homework after she realised that she had ashamed not only a pupil, but also his family when the boy, with the support of the father, failed at completing a homework assignment.

We all learnt much about teaching during the first year. The learning curve was steep, but our keen motivation to teach, alongside support from family and colleagues, confidence in our content knowledge, and most important, caring about the children, made us resilient and we continued in the profession. It really did not matter either we started our careers in an urban or rural city school in Norway, or in a kibbutz school in Israel. We experienced similar challenges and leaned on the same resources to find strength to make the first year into a learning year.

In preparation for this book, we listened to the stories of novice teachers from quite different settings: Australia, England, Finland, Israel, and Norway. We talked to several teachers, and selected two stories from each country to be included in the book. The teachers were interviewed using a semi-structured interview guide, which built on a book about Norwegian novice teachers, we had written in 2013. Moreover, we have made an effort to constantly updating our reading of relevant research literature. From the interviews, we wrote a narrative for each teacher, of which they approved. The teachers had all volunteered to participate in the project. The stories were analysed referring to recent international research literature. Each chapter consists of a short introduction to the national context written by well-known teacher educators and researchers in the respective countries, followed by the novice teachers' narratives. The third part of the chapter is our analysis with a theoretical perspective in mind. The book has 10 chapters like this. In the last chapter (Chapter 12), we discuss the narratives in a horizontal manner, looking for contextual similarities and differences.

2   Why Narratives?

Clandinin and Connelly (2000) claim that narratives are the closest we can come to experience. Narratives tell about life of teachers and students, and what they learn from experience (Clandinin & Murphy, 2009). Experiences are formed by the surrounding environment, it is an assemblage of a number of factors beyond the control of the narrator. The narrative is the subjective interpretation of experiences, thus the narrator's personality, emotions and environment are intertwined in the narrative. The narratives of these novice teachers are all coloured by their teaching contexts and who they are as persons. We believe that narratives as subjective truths are essential in trying to understand the challenges of novice teachers so we better can seek ways of supporting them as a group, and not least, individually.

> Narrative is the spontaneous genre teachers turn to when talking about their professional experiences. In using stories, anecdotes, metaphors, images, and so forth they provide accounts of their experiences and the meaning they have for them. As such the narratives represent interpretative constructions through which the storyteller creates coherence and meaningfulness in the endless stream of events and experiences. (Kelchtermans, 2016, pp. 34–35)

Other researchers have also used narratives to examine novice teachers' experiences. Schatz-Oppenheimer and Dvir (2014) used written narratives to explore three Israeli novice teachers' professional identity. They argue for the use of narratives (written stories) by first looking at how stories can contribute to professional learning, enhanced reflection and thereby support novice teachers in discovering the relevance of practice in the theory, and the relevance of theory in the practice. Their view aligns with the standpoints of two other Israeli authors, Orland-Barak and Maskit (2017) who point at the increased interest in using narratives as a pedagogical tool by way of involving re-storying and interpretation of one's own or others' experiences. An additional argument for using narratives is also discussed in Schatz-Oppenheimer and Dvir's (2014) article where they seek support in Bruner's work (1987) when they propose that narratives represent a reciprocate dialogue between the story and the teller, and become a means to organize the reality, which in the context of this book, is school and teaching.

Craig (2014) collected and analysed narratives from one novice teacher the first six years in her teaching career. Craig argues that narratives refer to temporality, sociality and place (Connelly & Clandinin, 2005), and is a story told in the present with a past as well as future perspective. The moment the story is told (written down) it is no longer dynamic, formed by momentary interpretation. It becomes static and public and thereby the reciprocal dialogue is gone. In a way we can say that a new dialogue develops between the narrative and the reader, who develops a subjective understanding of the narrative. The multi-dimensional time perspective is reflected in Craig's study in which she followed a novice teacher for six years. Craig examined the teacher's career trajectory over six years, and what started as stories to live by became stories to leave by when contextual micro-politics and pressure became unbearable for the teacher.

As already mentioned, in 2013 we published a book in Norwegian in which we present and discuss narratives of 12 novice Norwegian teachers (Smith, Ulvik, & Helleve, 2013). The book became popular among novice teachers and their school-based and university-based teacher educators. In the book we explain that the purpose for using narratives was to develop our understanding of the professional lives of teachers at the onset of their careers.

In the analysis of the narratives we started by looking for the essence of the stories meaning condensation (Kvale & Brinkman, 2009), and then we looked for a thematic thread. When writing the narratives we tried to arrange them in a chronological order to make it more reader friendly. Even though the experiences were told by the novice teachers, and the narratives accepted by them, the reader should keep in mind that we, the authors, wrote the narratives based on the rich information we had from the interviews. Thus, it is unavoidable that our own experiences and backgrounds might have coloured the translation from the interviews data to the written narrative.

3 First Year of Teaching: A Year of Learning

In the opening of this chapter we told about our own learning in our first year of teaching, and Caspersen and Raaen (2014) claim that during the first year of teaching, novice teachers seek to find their own ways of practicing teaching and are reluctant to ask for help when things are difficult. They do not want to show their lack of experience and often struggle alone. They are heavily engaged in a personal socialisation process of becoming a teacher, thus the working environment and relations with colleagues and the school leadership play a large role in the process of becoming a teacher. Alhija and Fresco (2010) argue that novice teachers in the first year expand their repertoire of teaching strategies, acquire practical knowledge, test their beliefs and ideas about teaching, and start forming their professional identity. In a study of 243 beginning Israeli teachers the above researchers found that the satisfaction with the first year of teaching was moderately high, and that mentors and colleagues contributed most to their learning process (Alhija & Fresco, 2010).

4   Mentoring and Collegial Support

Quite a lot of research documents the importance of mentoring during the first year (Smith & Ingersoll, 2004; Wang, Odell, & Schwille, 2008; Bullough, 2012, to mention a few). However, mentoring in itself is not enough, it is the quality of mentoring that matters, including the competence of the mentors, protected time for mentoring, and the openness of the mentee to receive feedback and guidance. The most common ways of mentoring is one-to-one mentoring, however, Kemmis et al. (2014) contend this view and argue there are various understandings of mentoring means, and that the field is poorly conceptualized. For example, in Finland most mentoring of novice teachers takes the form of group mentoring, whereas in Sweden and in Norway it is mainly individual mentoring. In this book our perspective is that mentoring is mainly for formative purposes, to support new teachers in their professional development and search for identity, Kemmis et al. suggest (2014) there are other purposes, such as the instrumental view of supporting novice teachers pass through the formal juridical requirements for probation (e.g. lists of standardized competences). This might be the situation for some of the novice teachers whose narratives are presented in this book. They have also experienced different forms for mentoring during the first year.

Buchanan et al. (2013) found among Australian novices that mentoring, not only individual mentoring, but also collegial mentoring as part of the workplace support, played an important role in reducing attrition from teaching in the first year. Collegial relations and support had a positive impact on the feeling of being included and socialized into the school community. In another Australian paper by Johnsen et al. (2014), the authors suggest that to promote early career teachers' resilience, four commonly views need to be challenged:

(1) focusing on the problematic rather than enabling behaviour, (2) seeing early career teachers as if they lack something, (3) not acknowledging that that social interactions and good relations lead to positive outcome for teachers, (4) the perspective that novice teachers are 'weak' manipulates instead of promoting interaction and supportive relationships. In other words, instead of having a negative perspective when discussing novice teachers, a stronger focus on their strengths might be useful. There are always two sides of the coin (Ulvik, Smith, & Helleve, 2009). Caspersen and Raaen (2014) claim that supporting novice teachers should be considered a collective responsibility in schools rather than the fate of the individual teacher. Strong and positive relationships in the work place are essential in reducing the challenges of the first year of teaching.

5 Main Challenges in the First Year of Teaching

There are, however, multiple challenges student teachers meet the first year of teaching, some of which are personally related, others are caused by contextual factors relating to the work place. Smith (2014) has grouped the challenges into four main categories. First, there are factors related to the personal circumstances such as maternity, family reasons, health problems. Second, teachers may be disappointed or even disillusioned by the reality of the teaching job. They often start teaching with an idealistic, not always realistic understanding of what teaching contains. It might be heavy workload, often caused by extensive 'out-of-field' teaching, which eats up leisure time in the evenings and weekends. Moreover, other reasons for the disillusion are large classes or difficult students, time pressure to get 'through' the curriculum, and being unable to be the kind of teacher they had envisioned. In addition, in some systems the demands of effectiveness measured in students' achievements and increased demands for documentation at the expense of time spent with students, are likely to cause emotional stress and burnout. Third, characteristics related to a specific school, e.g. low quality mentoring, harmful collegial relations, lack of support from leadership, and power struggle within the school, what Vanderlinde and Kelchtermans (2013) call micro-politics, are all common challenges in the first year. When the insecurity of repeatedly being offered part-time or temporary positions are added, it is understandable that induction to teaching are experienced as difficult. Fourth, as previously mentioned in this chapter, poor relationships with students (discipline issues), parents, colleagues and leadership of the school affect novices' experiences and emotions during the first year. The question is, how do beginning teachers find the strength to meet the challenges? In spite of the large attrition rates internationally, the retention rates are higher, and where do they find resilience?

6 Resilience

"Resilience is a mode of interacting with events in the environment that is activated and nurtured in times of stress" (Tait, 2008, p. 58). Day et al. (2007) claim that rresilience is a key factor to staying in the profession. It is assumed that the more resilient teachers are, the more likely they are to continue teaching in spite of external and personal challenges impacting their job. Resilience is a personality trait and affected by numerous external, as well as internal factors, thus it might be difficult to 'teach' people to become resilient. We support Gu and Day's (2013) claim that "The nature and extent of resilience is best understood as a dynamic within a social system of interrelationships" (p. 25), and we would like to add that these relationship differ from context to context and from person to person within the same context. From our work with novice teachers and supported by literature, we learned that sources for novice teachers' resilience can be illustrated by following figure (Smith, Ulvik, & Helleve, 2013).

A major source for beginning teachers' resilience seems to come from the students themselves, especially from students/classes they find difficult. If they succeed in developing positive and deep relations to the learners, the feeling of achievement strengthens the resilience. Novices feel responsibility towards these learners and not dot want to leave them to yet another teacher at the end of the year. Positive feedback from students has a strong impact on motivation from teaching. Socialization into the school culture and the community of teachers is another source for resilience. Positive relationships create an

FIGURE 1.1
Sources of resilience

atmosphere of trust, and the novice teacher feel confident to articulate their challenges and actively seek advice. The feeling of being included, and not being marginalized is important. The mentor plays a central role in introducing and 'sponsoring' the new teacher to the colleagues, and can positively contribute to socialization. Having a named mentor whose professional and personal knowledge and skills are trusted, who is available and interested in doing a good job as a mentor is highly appreciated by the novices we worked with.

During the first year of teaching the novices are developing their professional identity not only in terms of who they are (or want to be) as teachers, but also how they practice teaching in accordance with their own beliefs and the students' needs. This will naturally include trial and failure, and to be able to do this, novice teachers want to experience autonomy to try out new things. In school contexts, which allow for autonomy and accept failures as part of the learning process, also for teachers, novice teachers are likely to become resilient professionals. The fear of failing is harmful to any professional.

Motivation for teaching is a complex concept, however, recent international research suggests there are cross national common trends of teacher motivation (Watts, Richardson, & Smith, 2017). These are social utility, altruistic, intrinsic, and extrinsic as the least salient type of motivation. These types of motivation would also reflect the motivation of the novice teachers we have worked with, and the for primary school teachers social utility and altruistic motivation are strongest, whereas for secondary school teachers, which are more subject focused, intrinsic motivation is important. Regardless of the type of motivation, it contributes to novices' resilience to overcome challenges.

The final source for resilience mentioned in the above figure, is competence, mainly gained during teacher education. The feeling of being able to trust their content knowledge especially, strengthens the novices' feelings of being competent in the meeting with the students. It enables them to free energy to tackle problems related to pedagogical and disciplinary issues. Therefore, extended out-of-field teaching has a negative impact on resilience. When having to teach subjects not included in their education, beginning teachers spend much time familiarizing themselves with the curriculum, the subject, and in planning the teaching. This might easily cause burn out and lead to attrition from teaching (Du Plessis, Carroll, & Gillies, 2015).

7   Conclusion

We, as authors of this book, argue that the field needs to have a stronger research focus on sources of resilience for novice teachers, what makes them overcome difficulties and stay in the profession, instead of just looking at the challenges. We acknowledge that in the first year novices face multiple challenges, which we also have discussed in this chapter. However, if the purpose is to find ways to support new teachers to 'survive' the first year, we need to learn more about where they find strengths and seek support, and strengthen these factors during the induction.

The stories of the novice teachers presented in this book tell us much about the experiences of novices in an international perspective. They talk about challenges, but they also emphasize the many positive experiences they have, as we see in the various stories. We have tried to balance positive and negative emotions in our analysis of the narratives reflecting the beginning phase of the teaching career. We depend on the stories told by the novices themselves to understand what it means to enter a demanding teaching profession, and we are grateful to the participants for, so openly, sharing their stories with us.

References

Alhija, F. N. A., & Fresko, B. (2010). Socialization of new teachers: Does induction matter? *Teaching and Teacher Education, 26*, 1592–1597.

Bruner, J. (1987). Life as narrative. *Social Research, 54*, 11–32.

Buchanan, J., Prescott, A., Shuck, S., Aubusson, P., & Burke, P. (2013). Teacher retention and attrition: Views of early career teachers. *Australian Journal of Teacher Education, 38*(3), 110–129.

Bullough, R. V. (2012). Mentoring and new teacher induction in the United States: A review and analysis of current practices. *Mentoring & Tutoring: Partnership in Learning, 20*(1), 57–74.

Caspersen, J., & Raaen, F. D. (2014). Novice teachers and how they cope. *Teachers and Teaching – Theory and Practice, 20*(2), 189–211.

Clandinin, D. J., & Connelly, F. M. (2000). *Narrative inquiry: Experience and story in qualitative research.* San Francisco, CA: Jossey-Bass.

Clandinin, D. J., & Murphy, M. S. (2009). Relational ontological commitments in narrative research. *Educational Researcher, 38*, 598–602.

Connelly, F. M., & Clandinin, D. J. (2005). Narrative inquiry. In J. Green, G. Camilli, & P. Elmore (Eds.), *Complementary methods for research in education* (3rd ed., pp. 477–488). Washington, DC: American Educational Research Association.

Craig, C. J. (2014). From stories of staying to stories of leaving: A US beginning teacher's experience. *Journal of Curriculum Studies, 46*(1), 81–115. doi:10.1080/00220272.2013.797504

Day, C., Sammons, P., Stobart, G., Kington, A., & Gu, Q. (2007). *Teachers matter: Connecting lives, work and effectiveness.* Maidenhead: Open University Press.

Du Plessis, A., Carroll, A., & Gillies, R. M. (2015). Understanding the lived experiences of novice out-of-field teachers in relation to school leadership practices. *Asia Pacific Journal of Teacher Education, 43*(1), 4–21. doi:10.1080/1359866X.2014.937393

Gu, Q., & Day, C. (2007). Teachers resilience: A necessary condition for effectiveness. *Teaching and Teacher Education, 23*, 1302–1316.

Ingersoll, R. M., & Smith, T. M. (2004). Do teacher induction and mentoring matter? *National Association of Secondary School Principals Bulletin, 88*(638), 28–40.

Johnson, B., Down, B., Le Cornu, R., Peters, J., Sullivan, A., Pearce, J., & Hunter, J. (2014). Promoting early career teacher resilience: A framework for understanding and acting. *Teachers and Teaching: Theory and Practice, 20*(5), 530–546.

Kelchtermans, G. (2016). The emotional dimension in teachers' work lives: A narrative-biographical perspective. In M. Zembylas & P. A. Schutz (Eds.), *Methodological advances in research on emotion and education* (pp. 31–42). Basel: Springer International.

Kemmis, S., Heikkinen, H. L. T., Fransson, G., Aspfors, J., & Edwards-Groves, C. (2014). Mentoring of new teachers as a contested practice: Supervision, support and collaborative self-development. *Teaching and Teacher Education, 43*, 154–164.

Kvale, S., & Brinkmann, S. (2009). *Interviews: Learning the craft of qualitative research*. Los Angeles, CA: Sage Publications.

Orland-Barak, L., & Maskit, D. (2017). Cases as 'records of experience'. In *Methodologies of mediation in professional learning* (Chapter 4, Professional Learning and Development in Schools and Higher Education Series, Vol. 14). Cham: Springer.

Schatz-Oppenheimer, O., & Dvir, N. (2014). From ugly duckling to swan: Stories of novice teachers. *Teaching and Teacher Education, 37*, 140–149.

Smith, K. (2014, February). *One a teacher, always a teacher? Examining teacher attrition in a Norwegian and international perspective* (Application submitted to the Norwegian research council, FINNUT program). Bergen: University of Bergen.

Smith, K., Ulvik, M., & Helleve, I. (2013). *Førstereisen – Lærdom hentet fra nye læreres fortellinger* [The First Journey – Lessons learned from newly qualified teachers]. Oslo: Gyldendal Akademisk.

Tait, M. (2008). Resilience as a contributor to novice teacher success, commitment, and retention. *Teacher Education Quarterly, 35*(4), 57–76.

Ulvik, M., Smith, K., & Helleve, I. (2009). Novice in secondary school. The coin has two sides. *Teaching and Teacher Education, 25*(6), 835–842.

Vanderlinde, R., & Kelchtermans, G. (2013). Learning to get along at work. *Phi Delta Kappan, 94*(7), 33–37.

Wang, J., Odell, S. J., & Schwille, S. A. (2008). Effects of teacher induction on beginning teachers' teaching: A critical review of the literature. *Journal of Teacher Education, 59*, 132–152.

Watt, H. M. G., Richardson, P. W., & Smith, K. (2017). *Global perspectives on teacher motivation*. Cambridge: Cambridge University Press.

PART 1

The Australian Teacher Education Context

Introduction to Part 1: The Australian Context

John Loughran

1   Structure of Teacher Education

Teacher Education in Australia is offered at the undergraduate and graduate level. The undergraduate level includes the four year Bachelor or Education as a stand-alone degree which is most typically the programme designed for Primary (Elementary) teachers. Undergraduate double degree programmes are common for secondary teacher education programmes and increasingly so for primary education. The double degree is usually a mix of the cognate field (i.e., B.Sc., B.A., B.Mus., etc.) with an Education Degree (B.Ed.). The advantage of the double degree is that with overloading in enrolment, students are usually able to complete the double degree within four years thus receiving a qualification such as B.Sc./B.Ed.

Recent changes at the national level to move to a two year post initial degree qualification means that there are no longer any one year end-on graduate education programmes (e.g., Graduate Diploma of Education). The graduate (post initial degree) programme is now the Master of Teaching and is organized around an accelerated programme (with summer semester) so that it can be completed in 18 months and the standard programme which takes the full two years. The Master of Teaching operates at all levels from Early Childhood, through to Primary and Secondary Education. Finally, there is a growing trend for dual sector qualifications (i.e., Early Years/Primary; Primary/Secondary) which are becoming popular as students like the possibility of deciding after graduation the level of school teaching they would like to pursue.

2   Status of Teaching Profession

As with many countries, teaching as a profession does not appear to be as highly valued as it once was with the level of remuneration, political and public perceptions declining slowly over time. Teaching is an increasingly feminized workforce and entry scores vary across the university sector as is the case with many university programmes beyond teacher education, partly reflecting the supply and demand issues common to the sector. Entrance to university is determined on the final year of secondary schooling assessment outcomes which comprise a mix of internal (school-based) and external (exams) assessment approaches. All students who complete secondary school assessment (Years 11 and 12) receive a global score known as an Australian Tertiary Admission Rank (ATAR) with the top score being 99.95. The ATAR score is then used to determine a university's entrance score for each degree. Entrance into teacher education can vary from a minimum score of 85 (Monash University) to 50 (some regional universities).

Teaching is continually buffeted by the demands and expectations that are voiced through political rhetoric by which many social conditions are seen as needing to be 'solved' and that school is where that solution should be based. When that is not the case, teaching tends to be seen as partly responsible for not doing what should have been done. On the other hand, although the public perception may be critical of teaching, at a personal level, it is common for most parents to be happy with their school, their teachers and the education environment their children experience.

Novice teachers are increasingly under pressure. Recently the government has sought to introduce literacy and numeracy tests for graduate teachers and the certification system seeks to ensure evidence that 'standards' have been met through all teacher education programmes. On moving into teaching as a job, beginning teachers may experience well organized induction programmes, or (particularly if employed on a short term contract), receive very little support. Although there is recognition that induction is necessary, there is great variation across schools and schooling systems. At one level there may be a time allowance as a beginning teacher, a buddy system and fully organized mentoring structures, at another level a school may offer very little.

3   Employment

The job market tends to be stronger at the secondary as opposed to the primary school level. Beginning teachers in some disciplines (Maths, Science, Languages) tend to be in demand, and job opportunities are reasonable in rural/regional/remote areas. The Australian schooling system comprises Government schools (the large majority of the market), Independent schools (high fee paying schools often described as private schools) and Religious based schools (the Catholic sector being an education system in its own right). Job opportunities exist across all sectors and many teachers begin and end their careers in the system in which they are initially employed and gain tenure.

Because of the consistent demand for Maths, Science and Language teachers and the lower numbers graduating from these fields compared to many other teaching specialisms, there is a degree of out of field teaching (exacerbated if a school is not in a metropolitan area). However, it would be uncommon for out of field teaching to be experienced in a school in the final 2 years of secondary education. Most out of field teaching would be around middle school. Largely, the specialist teaching necessary for subjects in Years 11 and 12 is heavily dependent on, and staffed by, appropriately qualified teachers.

Teaching and teacher education in Australia is consistently and continually reviewed by governments of all persuasions and, in many cases, the constant attention to the work of teaching has caused a change in the public perception of the standing of the profession and inevitably has impacted student choice for a career in teaching.

CHAPTER 2

Carol's Story: Teaching Is Too Much Fun to Be a Real Job!

In my school there are more than five hundred pupils, divided upon twenty classes. The classes are fairly small. I have 20 pupils in my class, and I think at the most there may be 25–26. I used to be a grade three teacher, with general subjects like Maths, English, Science, Inquiry which covers humanities and all that sort of things, and then Geography. This year I am in grade six. I don't know what will happen to me next year, because it is just another twelve months contract that I am on. First I was on a twelve months contract, so I had to reapply for my job at the end of the year. I was told in the second last week of last year that I would get another year again for this year, which is another twelve months. And so I will have to apply again.

1   Why Teacher?

Both my parents are secondary school teachers. Actually that was how they met, in teacher education. Ever since I was in year 11 at school, every part-time job I had, I did after school care, I did holiday programmes, I did sewing teaching. Everything was connected to teaching. And I thought: "This is too much fun to be a real job". I also acted as a teacher for my sister. She is eight and a half year younger than me. So ever since she started school, I was walking her to and from school. And when I was at work experience in year ten in secondary school I worked in her school. I would go in and help with their classroom. Because there is such a big age gap, just watching her grow, I can even remember the day she was born. For me it was really good to follow all the milestones she passed. I like having that involvement with the pupils as well. Because my parents were teachers, I thought I might want to do something different. So I did a year of biological science and I found that teaching was for me. I really wanted to do it. So I finished that year and transferred to teacher education. And yeah – I just love it. So actually I have always known that I was going to be a teacher.

2 The Beginning

The first six months were extremely busy. I knew that it would be busy, but there is so much. It is almost like being a counsellor, the amount of social issues that the kids have: I did not realize how much time I would spend just helping them out with friendship issues and stuff like that. Getting to know how school works, as well as my pupils, the parents, even just the curriculum, I did not know where the things at school were kept. It simply took a while for me to wrap my head around. I came to school every morning, at least an hour before the kids, 7.30 and getting my stuff done in the morning, some days I was staying in quite late. I was trying to make sure that I did not fall behind in anything.

I was glad that there were five of us last year who were new at school. Four of us from the first year are still here, so that is kind of helpful. We all became friends and it wasn't just me on my own. In our school, at the start of last year, there was a mentoring programme that we were part of. The four new teachers were put together in two couples. I was Sam's peer and we had the same mentor. Our mentor was Henny. Both mentors were in their fifth year of teaching. I think there were four levels to it. Our two mentors then had a mentor who was Ada, an experienced teacher. And then above her was Jenny, who last year was our curriculum adviser and now at the moment she is our acting assistant principle. So you see it is kind of a layer. The study they are doing, I might be wrong, but as far as I understood it, was to provide support – trying to show that if new teachers get a lot of support in their first year of teaching, then it kind of drops off. This programme was meant to keep the support going, so that people with five years' experience got mentored by the experienced teachers, and they kept mentoring us for our first couple of years. Sam and I were supposed to film each other teaching and then have meetings with our mentor and give feedback to each other and reflect on it. That was really helpful as well. We observed each other and we discussed our experiences afterwards. So because I had to make videos with Sam and he filmed me, we observed each other closely. And then in my planning time I would go and observe other teachers teach and I always had Sam next door. There was a sliding door, so I could watch him and he could watch me, and we would also talk about our teaching and reflect on it. Henny sometimes watched the film and gave us feedback as well.

3 To Become a Real Teacher

What I enjoy most of all is to see that I can make a difference for my pupils. I had one boy in my class who had Aspergers, and at the beginning of the year it took me quite a while to build a relationship with him. I had been told about him from his previous teacher; about his behaviour and things like that. It took me quite a while to get to know him. But just seeing him grow throughout the year, and developing that relationship was fantastic. I think in the beginning, because I was trying to get to know him, I did not have really high expectations. But gradually as I got to know him I set really high expectations because I knew he could do it. I was quite tough with him. But the amount of work he produced throughout the year compared to the beginning was enormous. And I got really good feedback from the parents. His mum had tears in her eyes and said to me on the last day before vacation, she was just so happy with how his year had gone and he had such a good year. And he really liked me. Actually, I went on camp with him last week. It was just so good to see. I appreciated to learn that I can have an influence on challenging pupils, and I think they have an impact on me as well.

There is especially one experience that has influenced me and changed the way I look upon myself as a teacher and that relates to another boy in my class. At the beginning of the school year his parents had told me that they were close to changing schools, because they were not happy with the situation. They said they had decided to take him out of school if this last year was no better than the former. He did not have many friends and he did not connect to any of the teachers. He is quite mature as well, that is why I did not understand that he had problems with relations to other pupils. He is a lovely kid, but he is a bit quirky, and I think that he is reacting in a weird manner. His parents know that. His older brother, I think was our school's football-captain, and people expected him to be in his shadow. And I think because I was new I didn't know his older brother, so I probably looked at him another way. Within the first month the parents came and saw me and they said: "Ah, he is really happy at the moment. He really likes you. You ask him about his weekends and you know about him, you are making a connection with him". At the end of the year, I had his parents separately coming up to hug me. And they were all in tears. I was really happy about how the year had gone. I got really good feedback by the end of the year, also from the boy himself. He was so much happier and had new friends. It is nice to know that you are appreciated and you see the growth of the pupils and you know you have contributed to it. It was really, really good to see how the boy was better than he had been in the past, and he was doing so well in school. I think that because no-one connected with him made me conscious about making sure that I do connect with each of the pupils and getting to know their names. It did not take much to get to know him, but because I did spend that extra time just getting to know his interests and stuff it made a big difference to his year. Now I will always make sure that I take that extra time to each of my pupils.

The staff I work with has impressed me. They are really supportive and helpful. It has made a deep impression on me. I have been so lucky. I have some friends that have finished University, and they are also happy in their jobs, but they do not love it as much as I do. So I am sure that has to do with the staff and the school I came to. For example there are three grade six classes this year, and one of the teachers that I work with she has been kind of a mentor to me and so I have been joining her this year as well. It is good that if you need to combine classes and do something together or you need to split up into groups, you know that your colleagues are helpful and are willing to be flexible. We seem to be working really well together. So that has impressed me most of all. When I look back to the beginning of the year there is just so much stuff that you learn on the job while you are teaching. So I think I am also impressed with myself and the amount of stuff that I have learned throughout the past year.

4   High Expectations for the Future

Actually there is not so much I don't like. In the beginning some of the pupils struggled to be resilient and deal with their own problems, but a lot of them wanted the teacher to solve it. I think some of the parents also expected the teacher to solve their problems, instead of the kids learning to solve their own problems. So if I had to pick something, it would probably be that. It seemed to be most lunch times that I would spend 20 minutes just to work out friendship issues. I wanted the kids to figure it out, but they were not able to. I had parents coming in who asked me to solve a problem that had happened on the weekend with her daughter. I did not think that was my job because it was on the weekend and it was not even at school. It is things like that I like the least.

I have definitely learned that I should set high expectations from the beginning of the school year. Last year I was quite nervous. I didn't know that much and I was still trying to learn a lot about the school so I did not know what I could expect. But now, since I am at the same school, I know the staff and some of the parents in my class already. Now I want to make sure that I have high expectations from the beginning and set the routines as early as possible. I just want to build the positive relationships with the pupils as early as I can.

I know it is going to be busy. I am sure it will never be really quiet. But I think it is going to be fun anyway. There is a lot of stuff coming up that I look forward to. And I really like the group of pupils I am going to have this year. I am really looking forward to the next six months. I think it is going to be good.

5   What Can We Learn from Carol's Story?

5.1   *Motivation and Self-Understanding*

Carol has a very strong devotion for teaching as a profession. In a way she is born into the profession through her parents' histories as teachers. Apparently her devotion for teaching understood as supporting and taking care of others has been utterly strengthened through the close relationship she had to her sister who is many years younger. By the entry of teacher education student teachers often hold images of teaching from their own childhood (Calderhead & Robson, 1991). People who want to become teachers tend to be inspired by experience, by people they have met, and by parents and friends (Spear, Gould, & Lee, 2000; Roness & Smith, 2009). Within research on motivation for teaching a distinction between intrinsic, extrinsic and altruistic reasons for motivation is often made (Kyriacou, Hultgren, & Stevens, 1999; Kyriacou & Coulthard, 2000). While students who are extrinsic motivated are instrumentally oriented and focus on external reasons, those who chose teaching for intrinsic reasons are concerned with the satisfaction of teaching in itself. Altruistic reasons for becoming a teacher are grounded in teaching as a socially important profession based on a desire to help young people. Carol's reasons for becoming a teacher seem to be based on a combination of altruistic as well as intrinsic motivation.

5.2   *Carol's Self-Understanding as a Teacher*

Kelchtermans (2009) argues that the way teachers understand themselves is a key-element in the understanding of teaching. He chooses to exchange the term identity with the concept self-understanding interpreted as a process where the newly qualified teacher analyses and adds meaning to experiences and their influence on the understanding of the persons' self and image of self. The term refers to the person's understanding of self at a certain moment, as well as the ongoing process of making sense of new experiences. A teacher's self-understanding is made up through five components; self-image, self-esteem, job-motivation, task perception and future perspective. Self-image is a descriptive component based on how teachers understand themselves as teachers; an image that to a large extent is built on how the teacher sees herself through the eyes of others. Closely connected to self-image is the evaluative term self-esteem. The teacher's self-esteem is depending on her own appreciation of the job she is doing. Again this understanding will depend on interpretation of feedback from others. Carol mentions two cases that apparently have had a positive impact on her self-image and her self-esteem as a teacher. In both cases she has established a relationship and been able to support the pupils in new ways. The first event is connected to the boy in her class who has Asperger's syndrome and whose parents were about to move him from the school because no-body understood him. Carol has made a great difference in the boy's life and his parents are very grateful. In the second case she also treated the child differently from previous teachers and got very positive feedback from the parents. When the newly qualified teachers in this book were asked about episodes that have made an impression on them and perhaps even changed their perception of themselves as teachers, most of the cases they refer to are linked to situations where they are able to handle a difficult situation with pupil(s). They have a strong sense of mastering something that was difficult and maybe like in Carol's case something that somebody else has not succeeded in managing. This corresponds to other research claiming that obtaining good relations to pupils is what counts most for teachers (Flores & Day, 2006).

5.3   *The Professional Community*
Like many other teachers in the book Carol is impressed by the supportive and helpful staff she has become a member of. In fact, this is what has impressed her most of all. Kelchtermans and Ballet (2002) claims that fairly little attention is paid to the fact that new teachers not only are supposed to be leaders of a class-community, they are also supposed to be members of a community of other teachers. As a newly qualified teacher you have to adjust to an existing organization. You are supposed to find your place and if you are left on your own that can be a painful process. In Carol's school they seem to have an impressive way of supporting newly qualified teachers through a specific mentoring-programme. As far as Carol has experienced it, the idea is to give a lot of support to the new teachers the first years in order to avoid drop out. The newcomers were put in pairs. Sam is Carol's partner. These two are mentored by Henny who has five years' experience and who in turn is mentored by somebody else. According to Carol there are several layers and the more experienced teachers are mentors for less experienced. In education there is a growing understanding of the fact that mentoring is not only a concern for the newly qualified, but also for experienced teachers. Focus is shifting from the traditional one–to–one mentoring to collegial collaboration and an acknowledgment of the fact that participants in a group bring multiple perspectives (Hargreaves & Fullan, 2000; Heikkinen, Jokinen, & Tynjälä, 2012). Hargreaves and Fullan claim that mentoring needs to be transformed from something that takes place in pairs to an integral part of school culture in order to form strong relationships between experienced and newly qualified colleagues (Wang, Odell, & Schwille, 2008).

Sam and Carol are close neighbors with classrooms next door to each other and a sliding door that makes it possible to watch each other teaching. Apparently, they are encouraged to spend time on feedback and reflection. According to Hobson, Ashby, Malderez, and Tomlinson (2009) numerous studies have found that one of the most valued aspects of mentoring is lesson observation. There seems to be several aspects that are important in order to make observations valuable. First that the observation is conducted in a sensitive, non-threatening way, second that focus is on specific aspects of the observed teachers' teaching and third that it provides an opportunity for genuine and constructive dialogue between mentor and mentee. The fourth and final point is that effective mentors ensure their mentees are sufficiently challenged (Helleve, Danielsen, & Smith, 2015). When we listen to Carol we get the impression that she is confident with the collaboration she has with Sam. Apparently, they have a dialogue based on mutual respect, and they are supervised by Henny who sometimes also watches their videos and give feedback as well.

6   Conclusion

Talking with Carol is inspiring. In spite of the fact that she does not know if she has a job nest year she is full of optimism. She loves her profession. She was strongly motivated before she started her career and had been motivated from her childhood. Apparently the first year as a teacher has strengthened the motivation and belief in the fact that she has found the right profession.

References

Bandura, A. (1993). Perceived self-efficacy in cognitive development and functioning. *Educational Psychologist, 28*(2), 117–148.
Bandura, A. (1997). *Self-efficacy: The exercise of control.* New York, NY: Freeman.
Calderhead, J., & Robson, M. (1991). Images of teaching. Student teachers' early perceptions of classroom practice, *Teachers and Teacher Education, 7*(1), 1–8.
Hargreaves, A., & Fullan, M. (2000). Mentoring in the new millennium. *Theory into Practice, 39*(1), 50–56. http://dx.doi.org/10.1207/s15430421tip3901_8
Heikkinen, H. L. T., Jokinen, H., & Tynjälä, P. (2012). *Peer group mentoring for teacher development.* Hoboken, NJ: Taylor & Francis.
Helleve, I., Danielsen, A. G., & Smith, K. (2014). Does mentor-education make a difference? In H. Tillema, G. J. van der Westhuizen, & K. Smith (Eds.), *Mentoring for learning* (pp. 313–333). Rotterdam, The Netherlands: Sense Publishers.

Hobson, A. J., Ashby, P., Malderez, A., & Tomlinson, P. D. (2009). Mentoring beginning teachers. What we know and what we don't. *Teaching and Teacher Education, 25*(1), 207–216.

Kelchtermans, G. (2009). Who I am in how I teach is the message: Self-understanding, vulnerability and reflection. *Teachers and Teaching: Theory and Practice, 15*(2), 257–272.

Kyriacou, C. M., & Coulthard, M. (2000). Undergraduates views of teaching as a career choice. *Journal of Education for Teaching, 26*(2), 117–126.

Kyriacou, C. M., Coulthard, M., Hultgren, Å., & Stevens, P. (1999). Norwegian University students' views on a career in teaching. *Journal of Vocational Education and Training, 54*(1), 103–116.

Pajares, F., & Schunk, D. H. (2001). Self-efficacy, self-concept, and academic achievement. In J. Aronson & D. Cordova (Eds.), *Psychology of education: Personal and interpersonal forces*. New York, NY: Academic Press.

Roness, D., & Smith, K. (2009). Post Graduate Certificate in Education (PGCE) and student motivation. *European Journal of Teacher Education, 32*(2), 111–134.

Schunk, D. H., & Zimmerman, B. J. (2002). The development of academic self-efficacy. In A. Wigfield & J. Eccles (Eds.), *Development of achievement motivation* (Chapter 5). San Diego, CA: Academic Press.

Wang, J., Odell, S. J., & Schwille, S. A. (2008). Effects of teacher induction on beginning teachers' teaching: A critical review of the literature. *Journal of Teacher Education, 59*(2), 132–152. http://dx.doi.org/10.1177/0022248710731400

Zimmerman, B. J. (2000). Self-efficacy: An essential motive to learn. *Contemporary Educational Psychology, 25*(1), 82–91.

CHAPTER 3

Eric's Story: I Love the Spontaneity of My Profession

I am a general class-room teacher who teaches English and Maths as the main subjects. I have just started my second school-year with some of the pupils I had last year. But in Australia we normally switch the pupils around so none of the classes are the same from one year to the other.

1   Why Teacher?

Maybe for 12 to 13 years it was in my mind that I wanted to become a teacher. The main reason why I chose it is that my mother was a kindergarten teacher and I loved to be in her company and help her with her work. I loved the interaction with the kids. I really enjoy working with pupils and see them develop. It is impressive how much they look up to you, and respond to you and respect you. When I look at the pupils and think where they are in fifteen years' time, I hope I could have had a bit of influence on their lives.

I love to interact with them. Their personality is so impressionable. I think that is important for me. Doubtless, my parents' ability to guide me without putting pressure on me has helped me to find my way in teaching as a profession. I had a bit of trouble after I had finished high school. My parents just never, whatever I said I wanted to do, they said: "You choose. We'll be there to support you". But they always, I think they always wanted me to become a teacher. They always kept saying: Don't forget teaching. I finally decided after a break. I had two years off between finishing school and going to university. I moved away from home and did some other things and then finally decided that I should change my life. And I am glad I did. I am also glad that I had that time away from the school system and just had a bit of time for myself and for enjoying certain things before I was locked into a job where I have to be responsible five days a week, 40 weeks of the year.

2   The Community of Learners

During my first year there were five new teachers at the school. They all had their own mentor and then they also had the other people in their year level to help support them. I was given a mentor who had been teaching for about five years. I could go to him and ask him questions, get advice or just ask him about particular students and what to do. So he was my main mentor, but I also had the three others in the team who were there for support as well. We planned together and we had a team meeting once a week. They were very supportive. They always gave advice and offered things to do. If I needed a break then they would take my kids for some minutes and stuff like that. So that was very good. We were five newly qualified teachers this year. We had the occasional meetings, especially early with the assistant principal. She would bring us all together and just ask how we were doing. There was no real collaboration on a consistent basis. It was more that they made time for us to catch up at school. So that was the most important. Maybe once every eight to ten weeks. We were discussing strategies that the other newly qualified teachers had learnt at University that I didn't know. The five of us all went to different Universities. There were things that they had experienced in their placements that they had seen other teachers do. I think it was just really good to reflect together. We all became quite good friends. We went out for coffees, for lunch and we just relaxed and talked about it. And because we were all in a very similar spot, we could really help each-other and say: This worked for me, maybe try this, and this did not work. We could just really share our ideas, which was very useful.

3   The Beginning

Looking back I think I handled the first six months as a teacher fairly well. It was busy, but at the same time I think I felt like I did a lot of things that I did not really need to do. Looking back now, after another six months I think because I was not fully aware of what the job included I did not understand how much work I should put into it. So there was a lot of repeating myself and going over things I had done, and what was the best ways to be doing things? There was a lot of experimenting I suppose, a lot of walking in and going over what am I going to teach today. But at the same time it was extremely exciting. For a long time I had thought about having my own class, be able to set up my own rules and expectations. So it was extremely exciting, but at the same time it was nerve wracking. I often thought to myself: "Am I teaching them anything, do they learn anything, am I helping anybody?" However, I did not get overworked. Maybe the reason was that I took one day at the time. I think perhaps I spent too much time on tasks that were not worth it. I suppose I did too much of the "wrong" things and spent my energy on tasks that were not so important. In the moment it was difficult to see, but I can see it now.

4 The Teacher as an Artist

I just love the spontaneity of my profession. How different one day can be from the next. You never know what experiences the kids have had the night before. I enjoy it because every day can be completely different from the previous. The day may be horrible because one of the kids has not slept the night before, and he comes in and he is angry and upset and causes trouble. And then the next day, the classroom is perfect and everything runs so smoothly. So that part is pretty exciting. Because I can wake up every morning and think: Wow! What will happen today? And I also enjoy the freedom of it in a way. Because it is my class, I've got 24 pupils and I have a curriculum that I need to stick to, but I can sort of teach it in my own way. As long as I am getting the right outcomes it doesn't matter how I teach it. So I really enjoy the flexibility in the way that I can approach the actual teaching process. So what I enjoy most is to spend time with the kids and most of all when they achieve results that make them happy. It is extremely satisfying when one of my pupils is struggling on a topic and then suddenly is able to figure it out. When you explain something over and over again, you explain it in five or six different ways. And then finally they get it. You can see that they think "Oh! Yeah. I get it now" and they have a big smile on their face and things like that. It's a very rewarding part of the job, which is really nice.

5 Demands from the Authorities

The difference in the ability level of my students has been a real shock to me. In fact I was expecting a difference but the degree I have found it to be has been very surprising. I was definitely surprised, and still am surprised, by the difference in the ability levels between some students that are the same age, or one student that is older than the other student. I was not prepared for that. It scares me how different levels they can be on, even though they've been to the same school, the same system and the same classes. They have the same learning environment, but they're just complete opposites. So definitely, that has been a massive surprise to me. Every time I start a new year, I've got new kids, and I think: "How is it possible that they are so different?" However, it is easy to underestimate how much pupils know, and not appreciate what they actually know. It surprises me when we start talking about something new that you think they may not have heard anything about and there are pupils who know a lot and there are pupils who can really pick things up very quickly. In Australia we have a kind of national test that is called the Naplan. They do it grade three and then they miss a year in grade four and then they do it again in grade five. Then it sort of tracks their growth from grade three and grade five. That gives a standard school rate across Australia; for how well the students and schools compare to each other. Since this is my first time experience, I am not sure how it will influence me, but I guess the problem is that they always say "don't teach to the test". You want to teach the outcome, not to the test. However, you are kind of forced to, because it is in the start of next term. We are judged as teachers by how well these kids perform in the Naplan. So in a way it forces you to teach the things you know are going to be on the test. I know it is easy to change from traditional teaching and just do test practice. It feels important to do things like that to make sure that your kids are not the ones with the lowest score in Australia. It certainly stresses some of the kids out. I am sure many teachers are stressed about it as well, but I do not like to think too much about it and I am not too worried.

6 The Community

The way I have been taken care of at the school has made a huge impression on me. I am so satisfied with the way the staff at this school has made me feel welcome and not heaped any pressure on me as a newly qualified teacher. They have given me time to understand and achieve everything I am required to do and that has been very important for me. I have learned through this year that the best way to go forward is to ask as many questions as possible to clarify what is expected. I have understood that I should never be afraid to ask. There are people around that are more than happy to help with anything. So what has really impressed me is the collaboration between the colleagues. There is quite a few at the school that are really good. You would not believe just how much time they spend to help you out. They also spend a lot of time on planning together. My colleagues are such good team players. Particularly two teams that I have been part of. I have been really impressed at how well we can work together as a team and get things done. There are other teams throughout the school that have been frustrated with each other, because some teachers contribute and others are just lazy. But I have been impressed by how the teams I have been a part of have been able to collaborate very well.

7 I Did What I Felt Was Correct

There is one episode that I think contributed to change the way I looked upon myself as a teacher. I had a boy in my class who had severe autism. I learned from his teacher in the previous year that he had had many episodes where she had asked him to do something. And he just exploded and left the room. The teacher said: "You just have to let him go in to another room". But from the first time he did so I just said: "No, you have to stay in the classroom with us. I'm not letting you go. I expect the same from you as from everyone else in the class". I think because he was used to it from last year, he just continued to do it. I said: "No, you stay here. You need to be part of the classroom". He came back and sat down and continued to join in. I think that influenced my confidence level a lot because it made me feel like I had made a good choice, an individual choice. And even though I had heard something from an experienced teacher, I did what I found to be correct. So I think that has enabled me to feel more confident in making my own decisions and my own judgements based on what I feel at the time. Just because someone who has been teaching for fifteen years tell me what I should do, I don't have to follow it if I don't believe in it. That episode really helped me to understand something. I have discussed it with the experienced teacher previously. What she said would happen, did happen, and I didn't follow her advice. I did what I thought would work best and it worked. This happened quite early in the year, and for the rest of the year, he was much better. He still had occasional episodes, but he knew that he was not allowed to walk out. He sometimes walked two meters behind everybody else, but when I said: "No, you have to come back to the floor", he would turn around and come back. That was definitely an episode that has influenced me as a person and as a teacher.

8 Future Expectations

In future I want to become more confident, and most of all to be prepared to take risks. I will try not to get upset if things fail. Because it just mean you can learn from it and improve. If it does not work, so next time I will try another way. It just shows the power of reflection on things you have done. Just to reflect on a lesson, even ten minutes or five minutes when you think: "Was that the best thing to do? How could I do it differently next time?" And then being prepared to accept that you have made a mistake, and then try something new next time, but still have the same sort of confidence in yourself to try something else. I use recess and lunchtime. Generally it is my time to think about those things, because it is still fairly fresh in the mind. We have two hours class in the morning and half an hour break, and then an hour and a half and then an hour break, and then another hour and a half. I use those breaks to think

ERIC'S STORY

about what happened. And always, whenever I am at home I think about what happened, and sometimes I dream about it. I can wake up in the morning and the first I do is to think about my job. I think I am almost constantly reflecting on it. Even say after I have done five minutes of teaching that I thought was rubbish. I cannot believe I just did that, but now I know that it does not work and I will have to make sure to change it until next time.

What I don't like is the uncertainty about future jobs. Last year there was a lot of uncertainty about jobs at the end of the year. At the moment, we are just contracted for a year at the time. At the end of the year, even if the school wants to employ me again, I still need to apply for my job and go through the whole interview process. This is the normal procedure in the public school system but not in the private system. Once you become what's called ongoing, you get an ongoing contract with the school and then you are safe. There is no set time for this. It happens whenever some possibility opens up at the school. Some of my friends have become ongoing after two months in their job, just because they had spots at the school. They kind of want to attract people to this school, so they want to keep people around. Consequently, we had to apply for our jobs. There is a lot of stress and worrying about our jobs. We have to write reports at the end of the year, and we have to write transition forms. All of that is stressful enough without having to worry about having a job for the following year. But that is what the system is like. I most likely have to go through a similar situation at the end of this year as well. I really don't like this system. After all it is only two months at the end of the year, or a month and a half, but it is a long draining period. Only three of the five newcomers got jobs. Two of the others had to find somewhere else, because there were not enough positions at the school. The school had fewer classes, and some people were coming back from maternity leave. Two of the graduates lost their jobs and they had to find something else. Hopefully it will be easier in future. And by easier I mean having more things to draw upon, just from experience. There is still so much that I feel uncertain about. When I look at other teachers they can just walk into a classroom, and they have already done this lesson about ten times and they know what works. They can do the lesson without really having to think about it. So hopefully I continue to build that path. My pupils make a low score; they are a long way behind. I hope I can learn some really good strategies: How to deal with the really poor pupils that are sort of 12–18 months behind where they should be. I have got maybe five or six I think out of 24 in my class who are quite a long way behind. Hopefully I continue to learn the right strategies and the right way to differentiate teaching for all of their ability levels.

And so I have to apply for a new job.

9 What Can We Learn from Eric's Story?

Eric is deeply concerned with his profession as a teacher. He spends a lot of time reflecting on his experiences; alone and together with his colleagues. He says that the first he thinks of when he wakes up in the morning is his job, and it even happens that he dreams about it. Through the first year he has strengthened his belief in the fact that teaching is the right profession for him. His story tells about a novice teacher who loves to teach and who highly appreciates the community he has with other teachers; experienced as well as other newcomers. However, concerns about the national test Naplan, and worries about next years' job situation are challenges he has to cope with.

9.1 *Need for Support*

Like many of the other novices in this book, Eric appreciates the way he has been met by his colleagues and the positive experience it has been to become part of a learning community (Opfer & Pedder, 2011). The school has a mentor-system that he becomes part of. He feels confident and can ask all kinds of questions. However, what Eric underlines more than anything else is the community he has with the other newly qualified teachers in his school. Altogether they are five who are educated from five different universities. Eric appreciates the fact that they have different backgrounds and bring in new perspectives. The Russian philosopher and literary scholar Mikhail Bakhtin (1981) is concerned with the possibilities humans have for learning through differences. Eric says that his peers were good to reflect together with. They had different experiences from different placements where they had seen teachers acting differently. Teachers have to find their own way, but learning from others through reflection is an important way of learning. Eric does not hesitate when he is asked if there is any episode that has made a great impression and has made him look upon himself in a new way. From an experienced teacher he is told that he should let the boy with severe autism leave the classroom whenever he wants. The first time it happens Eric does the opposite of what he had been told. He tells the boy to stay because he should be part of the class. That decision turned out to be correct. Eric did what he thought was best in that specific situation. From this episode Eric learned that he is able to make right decisions on his own and that he can trust himself as a teacher. The episode Eric experienced may be characterized as a critical incident.

In relation to schools and teachers' careers, critical incidents may be "… highly charged moments and episodes that have enormous consequences for personal change and development" (Sikes, Measor, & Woods, 1985, p. 230).

Furthermore, critical incidents are often: unplanned, unanticipated and uncontrolled. They are flash-points that illuminate in an electrifying instant some key problematic aspect of the teacher' s role and which contain, in the same instant, the solution (Woods, 1993, p. 357). Such major events, which occur very rarely in most teachers' lifetimes, become critical only after the event. The criticality of an incident can be identified only after the consequences of such an incident are known as in Eric's case.

The fact that newly qualified teachers need a mentor is thoroughly documented in literature (Ulvik, Smith, & Helleve, 2009; Helleve, Danielsen, & Smith, 2014). However, Eric's story tells us about the great satisfaction it is to take a chance and to see that your decision as a teacher turns out to be correct without and even against advice from others. Teachers who experience to handle difficult situations become more open-minded to different ways of teaching and more closely connected to the profession (Hoy & Spero, 2005; MacBeath, 2012; Smith, Ulvik, & Helleve, 2013).

9.2   *Teaching as an Artistic Profession in an Age of Accountability*

Eric loves the spontaneity of his profession and the difference he experiences from one day to another in the classroom. Very vividly he describes the golden moments when his pupils understand and are able to figure out a problem. Eisner (2004) reminds us of the similarities there is between the profession as an artist and that of a teacher through several points. First, the teacher like the artist has to pay attention to many different operations simultaneously. Further artists and teachers have aims, but still have to be flexible and willing to change. Both professions have to acknowledge that form and content are inextricable and that knowledge is tacit as well as possible to express. Both professions also have to consider the relationship between thinking and available media and to be able to create experiences that contribute to further inspirations and motivation. Eric seems to love the situation of uncertainty where he has to be prepared but still open-minded to the situation in the classroom. Many newly qualified teachers, among them Eric enters the profession with a strong passion for teaching and a strong desire to help and support other people. Like Carol he has been motivated for the profession as a teacher since he was a child. He used to join his mother who was a teacher in kindergarten and he wanted to do the same as her. A wish to make a difference in other people's lives is an often recognized motivation for many teachers (Manuel & Brindlesy, 2005; Roness & Smith, 2010). However, what newly qualified teachers are met with is a school that is characterised by an increasing work-load, with demands to goal-attainment, paper-work and bureaucracy (Ball, 2008).

Consequently, Eric's experiences are not only positive. He is deeply concerned and surprised by the difference in ability level between pupils at the same age. He describes how the acknowledgement has surprised him. These experiences are linked to the external demands concerning accountability expressed through the national test (Naplan). He is told by others that he should not teach to the test. However, Eric thinks that he has to be aware of the test because he does not want to be the teacher of the pupils who are at "the bottom in Australia". The attrition rate among newly qualified teachers is high in many countries. Teachers' experiences especially the first year seem to be significant for their future professional career and positive experiences seem to increase the motivation to stay (Murmane, Singer, Willett, Kemple, & Olsen, 1991; Smethem, 2005; Roness & Smith, 2010). Buchanan (2015) finds that in an age characterized by accountability newly qualified teachers tend to adjust easier to external demands than experienced teachers. Instead of opposition against the system like for example to refuse to teach to the test, they find another job.

10   Conclusion

We don't know what will happen to Eric. He is in a very early stage of his career. He says that he loves his profession as a teacher, but he also says that there still is so much he feels uncertain about and that he envies the experienced teachers who can just walk into a classroom and know beforehand what works. One of the lessons he probably will have to learn if he is going to stay in the profession is the following:

> As a young teacher I yearned for the day when I would know my craft so well, be so competent, so experienced, and so powerful, that I would walk into any classroom without feeling afraid. (Palmer, 1998, p. 57)

Eric is uncertain of what will happen to his job next year. It is a pity if he leaves the profession. We need teachers like Eric!

References

Bakhtin, M. (1981). *The dialogic imagination.* Austin, TX: Texas University Press.
Buchanan, R. (2015). Teacher identity and agency in an era of accountability. *Teachers and Teahing: Theory into Practice, 21*(6), 700–719.

Helleve, I., Danielsen, A. G., & Smith, K. (2014). Does mentor-education make a difference? In H. Tillema, G. van der Westhuizen, & K. Smith (Eds.), *Mentoring for learning* (pp. 313–333). Rotterdam, The Netherlands: Sense Publishers.

Hoy, A. W., & Spero, R. B. (2005). Changes in teacher efficacy during the early years of teaching: A comparison on four measures. *Teacher and Teacher Education, 21*, 343–356.

MacBeath, J. (2012). *Future of teaching profession*. Cambridge: Educational International Research Institute, University of Cambridge, Faculty of Education.

Manuel, J., & Bridley, S. (2005). The call to teach: Identifying preservice teachers' motivations, expectations and key-experiences during initial teacher education in Australia and the United Kingdom. *English in Australia, 144*, 38–49.

Murmane, R. J., Singer, J. D., Willett, J. B., Kemple, J. J., & Olsen, R. J. (1991). *Who will teach? Politics that Matter.* Cambridge, MA: Harvard University Press.

Opfer, V. D., & Pedder, D. (2011). Conceptualizing teacher professional learning. *Review of Educational Research, 81*(3), 376–407.

Palmer, P. J. (1998). *The courage to teach. Exploring the Inner landscape of a teacher's life.* San Francisco, CA: Jossey-Bass.

Roness, D., & Smith, K. (2010). Stability in motivation during teacher education. *Journal Education for Teaching, 36*(2), 169–185.

Sikes, P. J., Measor, L., & Woods, P. (1985). *Teacher careers: Crises and continuities.* London: Croom Helm.

Smethem, L. (2007). Retention and intention in teaching careers. Will the new generation stay? *Teachers and Teaching: Theory and Practice, 13*(5), 465–480.

Smith, K., Ulvik, M., & Helleve, I. (2013). *Førstereisen. Lærdom hentet fra nye læreres fortellinger.* Oslo: Gyldendal Akademisk.

Ulvik, M., Smith, K., & Helleve, I. (2009). Novice in secondary school – The coin has two sides. *Teaching and Teacher Education, 25*(6), 835–842.

Woods, P. (1993). Critical events in education. *British Journal of Sociology of Education, 14*(4), 355–371.

PART 2

The English Teacher Education Context

Introduction to Part 2: The English Context

Jean Murray

Teacher education in England in the 30 years since 1984 has been subject to significant changes, as part of an ever-present focus on raising educational standards in schools.

The sheer scale of Initial Teacher Education (ITE) in 2014 in England is a significant factor in determining provision, with numbers of student teachers (now often called 'trainees') projected to be around 43500 in 2014/15 (UUK, 2014). With the exception of secondary shortage subjects, recruitment has been good in the last four years as a result of the economic downturn and consequent graduate unemployment. There are multiple 'providers' (a term that indicates organisations validated to 'train' teachers) and diverse routes into teaching, including employment-based route (EBITTS) – notably School Direct discussed in more detail later – and School Centred ITT schemes (SCITTS). These routes exist alongside and sometimes inter-woven with traditional study for one year Post Graduate Certificates in Education (PGCES) of 36 weeks duration or three or four year long under-graduate degrees giving Qualified Teacher Status (QTS).

There are also schemes aimed at particular groups such as Teach First (like the Teach for America programme on which it is modelled, this programme recruits only trainees with 'good' degrees) and Troops into Teaching (for ex-members of the armed forces). In 2013/14 there were more than 33000 entrants into teacher education (UUK, 2014).

Since the election of the Coalition government in 2010, there have been wide-ranging changes to schooling, with the implementation of the Free Schools initiative and the acceleration of the Academies programme.[1]

These state schools are now permitted to recruit untrained teachers, if they wish. There is also an 'assessment only' route by which intending teachers can apply for QTS through assessment against the eight current teacher Standards (Beauchamp et al., 2014).

The government has also implemented moves for further 'reform' of ITE by using school-led models of training and opening up the 'market' to new providers. The main instrument here has been the School Direct programme in which schools recruit intending teachers, provide the majority of their school experience and arrange any other necessary training towards QTS.[2] First introduced as a small-scale pilot in 2011, by 2013/14 25% of all ITE places were notionally allocated through School Direct (UCET, 2014), with 'the scale and speed of the growth' taking many in the university sector by surprise (UCET, 2014, p. 2) and making the scheme already a significant route into the profession. The impact of the scheme has been compounded by a revised and more rigorous inspection framework aimed at improving the performance of 'providers'. In a revised allocation system, universities are given some – usually reduced – student numbers, but guaranteed or 'core' places are only allocated to providers achieving 'outstanding' results in Ofsted inspections.[3] The results were that many universities without those results now rely on gaining 'training contracts' from schools under the School Direct scheme. The market-led model in use here may be seen as one of purchase by customer (the school) of an ITE programme from a service provider (usually but not always a university), sometimes following a process which resembles competitive tendering. Whitty (2014, p. 471) sees this situation as resulting from the 'neo-liberal combination of the strong state and the free market'.

Notes

1 Academies are independent state-funded schools that are managed by teams of co-sponsors. Free schools are independent state-funded schools that can be set up by interested groups such as parents, religious groups and education charities.
2 There are two sub-routes on School Direct: most trainees follow the basic route, as described above, but the School Direct salaried route offers older graduates the chance to work and be paid as an unqualified teacher whilst training.
3 The guarantee of places for these 'grade 1' providers only lasts until the next allocations round in 2015.

CHAPTER 4

Anna's Story: I Want to Share My Love of Languages

1   Motivation

I am teaching French and Spanish from year seven to year ten and have students ranging in age from 11 to 15. I am also a form tutor (which involves looking after and being responsible for a particular group of students and helping them with any problems). I have a total of eight different classes in French and Spanish.

I applied for the job and got it after my first job interview, which was not bad. It is an average achievement for mathematicians to get a job after the first interview, but not for language teachers. I just applied on a website. Usually when you go for a job interview in England, they walk you round the school; often they ask students to do it. Then they watch your teaching for either half an hour or a full hour. Finally, you have an interview with the head of languages, deputy head teacher and head teacher. You have a panel of three in front of you. It is a bit impressive and quite stressful.

I wanted to become a teacher because I love languages and wanted to share my love of languages with other people. I am not an office person and cannot sit in front of a computer all day to make more money for the company I work for. I need contact with people. So what I like about teaching is that it is never the same. I have some experience from teaching adults and from primary school, and I was a bit scared of working in secondary school. Now I like the contact I have with the young people, although as a teacher I have my ups and downs, but mostly ups.

2   The Pastoral Care

I like being a tutor; it is another side of teaching that is more pastoral. In my school, we have vertical groups, and I have 15 students in my group. They come to my room every morning. Then I register attendance and convey any administrative information to them about what happens after school. I see them again in the afternoon after the lessons. In theory we are supposed to have different activities like assemblies, sports or competitions. Sometimes I am supposed to do literacy activities with them. It is quite hard to do these activities at the end of the day, because then I do not want to be strict anymore. To be a form tutor

I am supposed to be helping students with anything. If they have an issue, they are supposed to talk to me first. However, one of the girls in my group hates me, and I do not know why. Before I started, her mum talked to the leader of my team and wanted her daughter to change tutor because she did not like me, and she had never met me before! The tutor who had the group before me told me about the girl, and told me to be careful because she hated everyone, and I should not take it personally. So I was prepared, in a way.

3   Characteristics of the School

The levels of literacy and numeracy in the school are quite below average. But what is good is that the value added is more than the national average. It is not a prestige or private school or anything like that. So the teachers are not really in competition to be the one that gets the best results, and they are quite approachable and friendly in my school. I have heard that in other schools they are not.

It is not so formal either in my school, as it often is here in England. You are allowed to have a piercing or a tattoo, but you should dress properly. Male teachers are expected to wear a tie, and the women wear skirts that reach below their knees.

Some of the students in my school are even a little bit more motivated for languages than in an average UK school, because it is in an area of London where many children speak different languages, mainly eastern Europeans. So they know from their own experiences that there are some benefits of speaking different languages, which is not a typical British attitude.

4   Support

As a new teacher, I am supported. But my mentor is head of a department and is very busy at work, so she does not have time to take care of the NQTs (newly qualified teachers) as much as I would have liked. But the other staff is very helpful. I am supposed to have a weekly meeting with my mentor, but it does not always happen. However, two weeks before half term I had a horrible class. I was about to resign, to be fair, and when I told my mentor about it, she stepped in and had a go with the students and helped me to deal with them. It was quite helpful.

During the year, we are observed by the mentor. I have had one observation already, but I have not received any feedback. Another colleague told me that the mentor should have given me feedback straightaway. Anyhow, we have eight standards in England and the mentors just tick them or not. I have to meet the standards to keep my job.

5 Ups and Downs

What I like best in my job is the social thing, dealing with people, which is quite tiring sometimes, but I know I do it for a good reason. I am not sure if my students will become great linguists at the end, but at least I am trying to open them to new cultures and new languages.

The period so far has been very quick and tiring, especially in the beginning, because I had to plan my lessons without knowing where to go. While the others had power points or exercises ready, I had to plan every single thing. In addition, I would like by Christmas to be on a better level in terms of behaviour management. However, I have eight different classes, and there is only one that really is giving me nightmares. The others are teachable.

Still, I am very tired at the end of the day and there is lots of stress. The last day I had two pupils who started to fight in my lesson and I had to physically separate them. One kid just pushed me and bashed me and I fell down. We have had behaviour management sessions, and there they said – that is in theory – do not take it personally. Do not answer back whilst the students are doing it. If you answer back, you are going to have a fight with them. Just try to go back to the rules, and when they have calmed down and you have calmed down, try to go back to the kid and try to discuss. That is in theory. And to pick the right battles. Many of the students have a difficult situation at home, and it is easier for them to take it out on the teacher than on the parents, who can smack them. When the student pushed me, I knew it was not on purpose; still I was a bit shocked. The boy was only 13 years old and I was much stronger than him. But I cannot touch him and should try to rule with my voice, not physical strength. A friend of mine got hit by a girl with the elbow in her chest several times on the same day. She was the one who invited me for a pint the Friday this happened in my classroom. And the head of my department asked me if I was okay. Afterwards the boy was excluded from his class for a day. We have this unit at school where students have to go for a day or more if they have behaved very badly.

I do also have good experiences. For example when I see my students in the corridor and they say, *bonjour* or *hola*, I think that is nice, that is warming. The day after the boy pushed me, I was on my bike and there were some of my girls from the same class in a café. And when they saw me they were quite exited ... ahh, there is our Spanish teacher! So it was nice to see that some kids were actually happy to see me after school.

To be a new teacher is like being on a roller-coaster. Some days I think I have good lessons, other days, that I have not taught anything. So I do not see a linear progression. During the week I have a heavy workload, but I am trying not to bring home homework. I work nearly twelve hours every day. I have to spend time on students coming back for detentions nearly every day, and on an Internet system where we have to report everything that has happened, behaviour issues and admin things. I know I work so hard because it is my first year, so next year I will know a bit more what I am doing and spend less time planning, and in terms of time management as well, I will be more efficient.

I still need to work on positive behaviour management. I need to work more on the praise rather than sending students to detention. When you are a new teacher, it is a bit stressful, because you would like everything to go perfectly. But then you get stressed and angry.

I am optimistic though when I think about the future, and you can progress, as well, if you want to in England. I can become a curriculum leader or I can go into the pastoral side.

6 What Does Anna's Story Tell?

Anna was lucky to get a job. She describes it as normal for teachers who want to work in London to go through several interviews and also that their teaching is evaluated. Consequently, it might contribute to her self-confidence to know that she impressed her employer favourably and is selected among other candidates.

6.1 *Subject or Student Oriented*

Anna has a vision. She wants to share her love for languages and open her students to new cultures. She works in an area with many students from the eastern part of Europe and perceives her bilingual students as more motivated to learn a new language than what she regards as common in Brittan. They know the benefits of speaking more than one language.

Her motivation for teaching, however, is not merely connected to teaching languages. She also wants contact with people and she wants variation. In teaching, she has it all. Researchers claim that especially secondary school teachers go into teaching because of affection for and interest in their subject discipline (Kelchtermans, 2009; Roness, 2011). Eventually the job becomes important in a broader educational sense. Then the teachers appreciate having an impact on a young person's life, and contact with youth becomes an important motivating factor in their job. Roness (2011) found that already during teacher education, the student teachers became aware of the meaningfulness of working with young people. Other researchers describe student teachers' beliefs either as teacher- or subject-matter-oriented or as learner-oriented (Rots, Aelterman, Devos, & Vlerick, 2010). Anna's motivation for teaching from the very start was related both to teaching her subjects and to working with students. She had actually worked in an office before she got into teacher education and deliberately chose to work with people. Timmerman (2009) found in a study that the best teachers were considered to be those who combined content knowledge with a human interest in the students, and concludes that content knowledge appears to be a prerequisite for good teaching. However, content knowledge is not enough.

6.2 *The Caring Role*

Bullough (2011) claims that the most important of all professional matters is how teachers care. To do this, they need knowledge about children and need to be attuned to children. Some have contended that care has been devaluated by the authorities in recent times (Ballet, Kelchtermans, & Loughran, 2006). Teachers' roles are described as having changed, having become more complex and as a result having challenged traditionally constructed identities (Day, Stobart, Sammons, & Kington, 2006). Interactions in schools are currently described as market-based and performance-driven. Teachers are overwhelmed by implementation requirements and their work demands are intensified. The development undermines the idea of teaching as a broader social mission (Hargreaves & Goodson, 2006).

As far as students are concerned, they need teachers who see them and their learning and accept them as they are (Rodgers & Raider-Roth, 2006). Otherwise, they may turn to negative strategies like acting out when they perceive that their teacher does not care about them. To be perceived as a person who is present, the teachers need to be aware of their students and their work. The teacher needs knowledge of the subject matter, the students and their learning. The teachers also need a repertoire of pedagogical skills. Furthermore, trust is essential to presence, and is created every day through interaction (ibid). Anna was what she referred to as a form tutor. The role implied that she met the same group of students every morning and afternoon and their meetings were not subject matter-related, but were oriented towards helping students in their learning process. She was responsible for the students' wellbeing, and she initiated diverse socialising activities for them. As a form tutor, it is the pastoral part of the teaching role that is in the forefront. Through conversations with students, she gradually becomes acquainted with them and appreciates them. Thinking about the future, she might either want to become a curriculum leader related to languages or go into the pastoral side of education. Through her statements, Anna expresses that she appreciates both her subject and the caring role as a teacher.

Nodding (2012) describes the carer first of all as attentive, a person who hears and understands the needs expressed whether it be resolving an academic problem or something else. It is easy to assume students' needs. Teachers should watch and listen and primarily be attentive. Nodding states that a caring relation has both cognitive and affective dimensions and that listening is at the heart of caring for human others.

Anna relates some situations in which she struggles with her students. She mentions a horrible class and a girl who said that she hated her even before they had met, and once she experienced a dramatic situation where a student pushed her. In the first case her mentor stepped in and put things straight. In the second case, she was told beforehand that this was what that girl was like, and in the last case, she was told not to take it personally. Anna also got some general advice from some behaviour management sessions, and the boy was excluded from class for one day. We will argue that the help Anna got was related to taking control. She was supported by others taking over, either her mentor or a unit to which she could refer the student. It is unquestionably helpful for Anna not to be left alone in difficult situations. Furthermore, in the English school system there might be more hierarchy than, for example, in the Norwegian system. Only the different dress codes explain a difference. In Norway, it would have been perceived as a defeat if someone else stepped in and straightened out a situation involving students. However, Anna got no help in establishing or maintaining a good relationship from a caring perspective. Why would a girl hate a person she does not know? What will happen the next time with a horrible class? And what kind of relationship did she develop to the student that bashed her? Caring means being attentive and trying to be receptive to the needs of those whom one are caring for (Colnerud, 2015). Care demands reciprocity. Even though Anna got help to manage her teaching situation, one might question whether she was supported when it comes to caring and establishing a positive relationship. Following Noddings' conception, caring means to listen, and as far as we know, Anna was not encouraged to listen to students in any of the difficult cases. She was also left alone in processing the events – except for her friend who invited her for a pint.

6.3   *Being on an Emotional Roller-Coaster*

Anna describes teaching as being on a roller-coaster. We find the same description in a study among new teachers in Scotland (McNally, Blake, Corbin, &

Gray, 2008). The teachers in the study perceive that entering the teaching profession entails emotional labour. The formal standard for teaching does not seem to be helpful. What is perceived as useful is informal support from people in the teaching environment. The researchers claim that it is the emotional and relational dimensions of teaching that come to the fore in the initial phase of teaching. What is important is to be accepted as a teacher by students and colleagues. Consequently, it is not enough to be given a mentor; the whole school should be responsible for including the new teacher. The Scottish researchers conclude that new teachers need empathetic support to release their individual qualities.

Others also refer to emotions as part of being a teacher (Flores & Day, 2006). Newly qualified teachers invest a lot emotionally. Thereby they also might easier experience negative emotions when their practices are challenged, and they do not experience trust and respect (ibid). Most teachers survive their first year in the profession and want to continue as teachers. However, to strengthen teachers' resilience, Gu and Day (2007) recommend focusing more on positive qualities and strengths. Positive emotions are more durable, and it is the absence of positive experiences that undermines teachers' commitment (ibid.; Morgan, Ludlow, Kitching, O'Leary, & Clarke, 2010). Even if the emotional part of teaching is recognized in the research literature, Jakhelln (2010) found in a Norwegian study that emotions are neglected in novice teachers' work and that their emotions are not used for development and learning. An implication of the study is to perceive emotions as a positive source of novice teachers' development that may foster learning.

6.4   *Being Supported*

In England, novices are normally given an appointed mentor and some additional time for professional development. Even though Anna got a mentor, the mentor was busy and had little time for meetings. As a result, the support Anna got from her was limited. In England, mentoring also implies assessment, and there is a set of prescribed induction standards and guidance for mentors (Harrison et al., 2006). New teachers are supposed to be assessed by their mentor six times during the year. Anna has been assessed, but has not received any feedback. She explains that the mentors just tick the standards. For Anna it is important to know if she meets the standard, because keeping her job depends on it. Researchers found that because of fixed standards, mentoring has predominantly a technical and practical focus (ibid). For Anna that might be the case, but the other English teacher in this book, Owen, had a very different experience.

Not only newly qualified teachers have to follow a standard in England. To ensure quality teaching, there is a rigorous inspection framework, The

Office for Standards in Education, Children's Services and Skills (Ofsted). The framework focusing on teachers' skills as expressed in the Teachers' Standards (Department for Education, 2013). Schools, as well as individual teachers, are inspected and measured on a graded, four-step scale (outstanding, good, requires improvement, inadequate). How often a school is inspected depends on the grades they get. The aim of the inspections is to improve teaching. When it comes to Anna, she explains that her colleagues are approachable and friendly *because* they are not a prestige school and therefore are not in competition to get the best results. Competition might work against cooperation. From Anna's perspective as a new teacher, she does not see an advantage in being in a prestige school. The other English teacher in the book, however, has a different experience.

7 Conclusion

Anna's view of the future is optimistic. She has had her challenges, but they seem to be isolated episodes. She concludes that her experiences are mostly positive. She explains that it is hard work to plan everything for the first time without any experiences to draw on, but she chooses a positive approach. Most of her classes are positive and gradually she will manage. She accepts that she encountered some challenges initially, but she does not make an issue of it.

References

Ballet, K., Kelchtermans, G., & Loughran, J. (2006). Beyond intensification towards a scholarship of practice: Analysing changes in teachers' work lives. *Teachers and Teaching: Theory and Practice, 12*(2), 209–229.

Bullough, R. V. (2011). Ethical and moral matters in teaching and teacher education. *Teaching and Teacher Education, 27*(1), 21–28.

Colnerud, G. (2015). Moral stress in teaching practice. *Teachers and Teaching: Theory and Practice, 21*(3), 346–360.

Day, C., Stobart, G., Sammons, P., & Kington, A. (2006). Variations in the work and lives of teachers: Relative and relational effectiveness. *Teacher and Teaching: Theory and Practice, 12*(2), 169–192.

Department of Education. (2013). *Teachers' standards.* Retrieved March 8, 2016, from https://www.gov.uk/government/publications/teachers-standards

Flores, M. A., & Day, C. (2006). Contexts which shape and reshape new teachers' identities: A multi-perspective study. *Teaching and Teacher Education, 22,* 219–232.

Gu, Q., & Day, C. (2007). Teachers' resilience: A necessary condition for effectiveness. *Teaching and Teacher Education, 23*(8), 1302–1316.

Hargreaves, A., & Goodson, I. (2006). Educational change over time? The sustainability and nonsustainability of three decades of secondary school change and continuity. *Educational Administration Quarterly, 42*(1), 3–41.

Harrison, J., Dymoke, S., & Pell, T. (2006). Mentoring beginning teachers in secondary schools: An analyses of practice. *Teaching and Teacher Education, 22*, 1055–1067.

Jakhelln, R. (2010). Early career teachers' emotional experiences and development – A Norwegian case study. *Professional Development in Education, 37*(2), 275–290.

Kelchtermans, G. (2009). Who I am in how I teach is the message: Self-understanding, vulnerability and reflection. *Teachers and Teaching: Theory and Practice, 15*(2), 257–272.

McNally, J., Blake, A., Corbin, B., & Gray. P. (2008). Finding an identity and meeting a standard: Connecting the conflict in teacher induction. *Journal of Education Policy, 23*(3), 287–298.

Morgan, M., Ludlow, L., Kitching, K., O'Leary, M., & Clarke, A. (2010). What makes teachers tick? Sustaining events in new teachers' lives. *British Educational Research Journal, 36*(2), 191–208.

Noddings, N. (2012). The caring relation in teaching. *Oxford Review of Education, 38*(6), 771–781.

Rodgers, C. R., & Raider-Roth, M. B. (2006). Presence in teaching. *Teachers and Teaching: Theory and Practice, 12*(3), 265–287.

Roness, D. (2011). Still motivated? The motivation for teaching during the second year in the profession. *Teaching and Teacher Education, 27*, 628–638.

Rots, I., Aelterman, A., Devos, G., & Vlerick, P. (2010). Teacher education and the choice to enter the teaching profession: A prospective study. *Teaching and Teacher Education, 26*, 1619–1629.

Timmerman, G. (2009). Teacher educators modelling their teachers? *European Journal of Teacher Education, 32*(3), 225–238.

CHAPTER 5

Owen's Story: Empowering Students

I guess that I became a teacher because of my very positive experiences of education. I had very inspirational teachers and realised how much of a difference a teacher can make in somebody's life. Before I did my PGCE (postgraduate teacher education) year, I worked a few years as a special needs worker, and now I have a probationary year you have to pass to get a permanent position. But I think the failure rate is very low, really. The head teacher is the one who signs off if you have passed, but generally, it is the induction tutor that will assess you throughout the year and write a report and decide whether you pass or fail.

1   My Job

I teach sociology and health and social care. Health and social care was not a choice, but for some reason it is given to every teacher in the schools in the UK. I just find sociology very empowering for young people. I think it is really useful to understand the world around you.

In my PGCE, my training year, we had two placements, around two months each. I had my second placement in this school. I really enjoyed the school and think they liked me as well. They told me that they were looking for a sociology teacher and that I should apply. It seems to be difficult to find a job that maybe is perfect for you, so I was lucky to get this job. Some teachers have to teach a subject that is not their first subject. A friend of mine, for example, teaches majority history and psychology, but he is a sociology teacher and has to compromise.

In my job, I teach sociology majority, and only in six form, which is years twelve and thirteen, ages sixteen to eighteen, college effectively, which is very nice. I have four sociology classes and two health and social care classes. In year twelve, my classes have around thirty pupils, which is unusually large for a college class. Six to twelve kids is what I am used to, and it is much more reasonable to teach that number of children, because the subject is very content heavy. It is quite deep learning you have to do at sixth form. So to assess and to keep an eye on the kids when there are thirty of them in the class is difficult. I think that sociology, especially, is a subject you can make very interesting and accessible to young people and hopefully spark their interest.

2   Likes, Dislikes and Aims

The part of my job that I like best is being with the kids and I really enjoy planning lessons. As a teacher, you take a lot of work home with you, but I do not mind sitting at home planning lessons. I think that is really enjoyable and quite a creative sort of process. You always consider it, and sometimes you just have ideas for lessons. Planning and teaching a lesson and seeing progress in the kids and just making children happy is quite nice. Being with the kids is a big very rewarding part of the job, certainly.

The most challenging aspect, I find, is the kids who do not really want to learn or are not particularly interested. And I find it challenging to encourage independence. In education in the UK, I will say that children are spoon-fed when they are younger. They are given information. But you cannot tell them all the information they need. They have to find out that information themselves, which is a very important skill for the wider world when they leave education or continue studies at university.

Part of the job I do not like would be assessment. I can see that assessment is a vital part of teaching, and you need to know where your kids are. But I think that using trained teachers who are not trained examiners is a mistake, frankly. I think that assessment should be carried out outside the organisation, and you should be given the results as a teacher. I mean, obviously you are continually assessing kids in the class. You are marking their books, but there should also be assessments that are done outside, because how reliable is your assessment going to be when they are your own children, and when you have not been trained in examination techniques, not been trained in assessment for learning, formative assessment or summative assessment? The children will be assessed by someone outside at the end of the year, but I think they should have been assessed by someone outside once a term, at least. That could have given you very reliable feedback on their essays. I am not saying that teachers cannot do it. But I think it is very time-consuming and we have not been trained as examiners.

Especially in sixth form, it is about facilitating learning. You provide them with information, but you do not necessarily spoon-feed it to them. You let them make up their own minds. You make sure that the information is out there, and you give them clues about where it is, but you do not just give it to them and stick it in a book for them. They need to do their own sort of thing and to be able to evaluate information. I am struggling with one of my year twelve classes. If you are there telling them, dictating what they need to write down, they do it. But if you tell them, 'here is the information, go and find out', they will not do it. So making them do it is a struggle. However, I think that that is part of growing up.

I definitely have enjoyed working as a teacher. There are long hours and lots of work, but I have had other jobs where I have worked long hours, and I do not have a problem with hard work. I have enjoyed it. The kids are amazing, and it is a very rewarding job. It sounds cheesy, but I don't mind saying so. However, I have less time for socializing, and during the week I would not see anyone and work probably ten to eleven hours a day, and in the weekends, a couple of hours on Sundays. When I arrived, my tutor said that I should try not to take work home, so I try to stick to that and rather stay in school longer and get it done here. Part of what takes up a lot of my time is planning lessons. So once you have a resource for the lessons that is always a big time-saver, I imagine.

The feeling of teaching a lesson where every child walks out of the room quite happy is an amazing experience. A lesson that really works well and is active and all the kids are engaged and they will talk about it after the lesson in a very positive way – that is a very positive experience. In those lessons, the kids are involved and having fun, which is a big thing. I find it very difficult to consistently teach lessons that are very fun for the kids and are also very informative. You have to find a balance. Because you could do the fun stuff all the time, but it has to be linked to the curriculum.

I think teaching sixth form, the intellectual stimulation is very rewarding, you can build sort of strong bonds with the kids, and you can challenge them more. I think it is a very nice age to teach.

The biggest thing I have learned has been making sure that every child in the class is progressing; I found this challenging. You notice some kids and you see other kids melting into the background. That is not accepted in this school. So it has been very useful to be taught how to keep the assessment going to make sure that every child is reaching their potential, enjoying their learning and feeling happy with their experiences.

3 The Support

As a new teacher I have a tutor who oversees all the trainee teachers. We have two weekly meetings, an hour each, where we discuss various issues. So the support in this school is excellent, I have to say, very good. They spend a lot of time and effort making sure you are okay. And I know that friends and people who passed the course at the same time as I did have very little support in other schools. There they just let them get on with it. Here we have ten percent less teaching hours and we are observed twice every half term, so twelve times over the year. To be observed is partly good for the feedback and partly it keeps you on your toes, so to speak. You have to keep your lessons fresh and want to try out new ideas. Even when you are not being observed you think about what you are going to do and how you can improve your lessons.

There are around twenty NQTs in total in the school and also a large number of trainee teachers as well. It is a big group, but the school is well known for retaining their staff and they are known for being a good school to train in. I think they like to have a young staff because young teachers have to work hard.

In the mentoring group, we focused on how to deal with gifted and talented students one week. Special education and needs will be focused on another week and formative assessment can be one week. So we always have a focus and bring with us resources and ideas. It is really useful.

At the beginning of the year, the tutor had an overall timetable and asked us if there was anything we would like to add. If someone had ideas or a weakness they wanted to concentrate on, they could put that in, and then we had a timetable for the whole year. We bring resources to show what we are doing and read some chapters in a book, but there is not much preparation. I have been observed quite a lot and keep all the resources from my observations. In the end of each half term, we have to write a mini-essay about how we are doing. We also have a meeting with the tutor where we have to decide targets, and wherever we have met our targets from the previous half term. These reports amount to a lot of paperwork.

4   My Learning Outcome and Future

Last year I was surprised by how difficult it is to be a teacher, and how hard teachers work and how much folks go into it, so in my training year there were quite a few surprises. This year, one surprise is how much pressure there is and how much that affects relationships in schools and sometimes does not bring out the best in people.

Starting to work as a new teacher, a big thing is the inconsistency. I am in contact with the people I trained with last year and they are having very different experiences their first year of teaching, and it worries them. I am very lucky to be in training, but many other people are not. To become a very good teacher takes much more than a year and I think you need to be supported and nurtured.

I do not want to generalise, but the people I know who are not supported are people in academies.[1] The academies put a lot of pressure on their staff. They sometimes have a tutor or someone who is in charge and looking after them, but they would not have the time or the knowledge or the skills to do a good job of it. So that inconsistency is worrisome, because I feel that they perhaps would not reach their full potential because they are not given that support.

A lot of teachers leave, maybe fifty per cent leave after the first couple of years, which is very surprising. Maybe the cause is that they are not supported in their second year as much as they were in their first year and find it difficult.

In the UK, there are many changes occurring in education that I am not necessarily keen on. We are going back to the old school method of assessment, very much driven by targets. We are going to start having performance-related pay. Then the pay will be linked to how your kids are doing, which I can understand the logic behind, but I do not think it makes much sense. So if these changes continue to occur, I am not sure if I will stay in education.

If I continue, I would quite like to be head of department. And the idea of free schools is a dream. To be able to get a group of teachers to open a small school and be involved in a small cooperative, I think that would be a lovely opportunity.

5   What Does Owen's Story Tell?

5.1   *A Demanding but Rewarding Job*

Owen was lucky to get a job in one of his placement schools and was even encouraged to apply. In the school, he teaches the eldest students and describes it as rewarding and intellectually stimulating. From previous experiences as a student, Owen understands how much impact a teacher can have on students' lives. Being a teacher himself, he also wants to make a difference.

As the other teachers in this book, Owen enjoys being with students, but he also mentions planning lessons as an enjoyable and creative process. Planning lessons is not simple, and as Owen explains, it demands constant attention. Loghran (2010) describes teaching as complex and messy and presents in a book what expert teachers do. Some of the issues he mentions are as follows:

Expert teachers:
- Addresses prior knowledge
- Use time for students processing and elaboration
- Create links to prior knowledge
- Translate to different forms of representation
- Create synthesis
- Talk about learning

Some of these issues need to be improvised, but some can be planned or at least thought through beforehand. However, the different actions imply that teachers know their subject as well as their students, and dialogue seems important. The way a dialogue develops can never be planned, and facilitating rich classroom conversation is demanding without prior experience. It could be a good idea for new teachers to limit the time span for these conversations initially and expand them gradually. Furthermore, Owen explains how he always considers his teaching and sometimes has ideas for lessons. Following up good ideas and not teaching the same thing every lesson can be important to maintain students' involvement. "... it is from surprise that we are most likely to learn something", Eisner claims (2002, p. 8). However, for new teachers without a repertoire of methods it can be difficult always to come up with good ideas. Then it is safe to teach as you have been taught or to stick to methods where the teacher experiences being in control (Smith, Ulvik, & Helleve, 2013). New teachers likely benefit from cooperating with experienced teachers and get access to their ideas and experiences, and from having time for building up their own repertoire of teaching.

Teaching implies, for Owen, long hours and a lot of work, but he accepts it and tries not to bring work home. He thinks that when he has worked out a resource for the lessons, it will be easier the next years. Dealing with a heavy workload seems to be common for new teachers (Mansfield, Beltman, & Price, 2014; Smith, Ulvik, & Helleve, 2013), but what is regarded as heavy depends on what one compares with. Nevertheless, too heavy workload is one of the key reasons for new teachers to leave the profession (Kyriacou & Kunc, 2007).

Another aspect with which Owen struggles is his school's requirement that he ensures that all his students are making progress. In Owen's case he is supported in making sure that students reach their potential, but despite this support, it is not easy to fulfil the demand. He says that some students seem to melt into the background. A challenge for teachers is to deal with many at the same time. For new teachers who have a lot to learn, it might be difficult to get an overview of a crowded classroom. Owen discovers how challenging it can be to see each student when there are 30 of them in one class. Teachers are expected to treat every child fairly, but fairness related to equity, need and merit are often complex (Colnerud, 2015). There is sometimes a dilemma between attention to the needs of an individual student and commitment to the group as a whole, and teachers may feel inadequate as carers. Colnerud (2006) recommends that caring sometimes needs to be complemented by justice. It is impossible to cover all needs, and the teacher should be conscious about sharing time with all the students.

5.2   *Assessment*
Assessment is one of the things Owen does not like. He knows that formative assessment is an important part of teaching, but assessment is time

consuming and he feels that he is not sufficiently prepared. He thinks that assessment should be done by someone outside the organisation at least once a term (three times a year). That would provide him with reliable feedback. In our research, we found that assessment is a common challenge the first year in teaching (Ulvik, Smith, & Helleve, 2009). Teachers do not feel prepared for assessment and it is intimidating to be responsible for something that is so important for a student's future (Smith, Ulvik, & Helleve, 2013). We learned from novice teachers that when it comes to assessment, it is helpful to cooperate with experienced teachers. Furthermore, based on our research, we recommend that assessment becomes an important issue in induction programmes. It is necessary to have knowledge about assessment and it needs to be developed in cooperation with others. New teachers should not be left alone to assess students. However, we do not agree with Owen that the solution is to leave assessment to someone outside the organisation several times each year, and we do not believe that assessment would thereby be more reliable. Not only students need to be empowered, but also teachers. Owen's aim in his subject included fostering critical thinking, and that is not easy to measure.

5.3 *Empowering Students*

Owens main subject is sociology, and he emphasises how empowering the subject is for young people. He describes the subject as content heavy and that it presupposes deep learning. While surface learning might enable repetition of content, deep learning is about understanding and might imply elaboration and hard work. To achieve deep learning, students should be allowed to go deeply into things by concentrating on some chosen topics. Klafi (2002) recommends concentrating on the key questions in a society. Although deep learning can be challenging, Owen thinks that it is possible to make the subject accessible and interesting to young people. He wants his lessons to work, that the students are engaged and learning, and that they are happy. However, here he encounters a dilemma. It cannot be fun all the time, and he states that one needs to find a balance between lessons that are fun and those that are merely informative. Young (2013) has discussed the relation between the learner and the curriculum. He argues that curriculum theory cannot begin from the learner, but from the learner's entitlement to knowledge. It is the teacher's responsibility to transmit knowledge, but also to enable students to build on that knowledge and create new knowledge. Young claims that programmes based on interests may make students happier, but they will deny students access to knowledge they need to progress.

Owen wants to facilitate access to important knowledge and empower students, but finds it challenging to encourage independence. He describes teaching in England as spoon-feeding. He wants his students not only to be given information, but also to find out things by themselves and be able to make up their minds and evaluate information. He describes being independent as an important skill for students in their lives in general. School for him means educating students for life, not only for working life. Eisner (2004) claims that students need to be able to judge by themselves; in the world outside school, there will be no teacher to guide them. He proposes that education can learn from the arts about practice of education (Eisner, 2004). While there are correct empirical answers in terms of spelling or mathematics, one makes judgements in the arts without set rules. In the world outside school, there are no single correct answers to questions or clear-cut solutions to problems. Therefore, Eisner argues, uncertainty needs to have its proper place in schools Owen experience that students often prefer to be told rather than to think for themselves. He sees it as part of growing up to be able to find and evaluate information, and even if he struggles he holds on to his vision.

It can be confusing for students to deal with uncertainty and for the teacher to promote critical thinking. Nussbaum (1997) reckons knowing alternatives is a premise for critical thinking. Schools should educate people who can operate as world citizens with sensitivity and understanding. The best education then, she argues, is one that equips citizens for genuine choices. She quotes the stoics who hold that "we can see ourselves and our customs more clearly when we see our own ways in relation to those of other reasonable people" (p. 59). We should not think that something is best because it is our own, but be willing to doubt the goodness of one's own way (ibid.). Following Nussbaum, teachers should present alternative perspectives and give students access to what is beyond their own experiences and everyday life.

5.4   *The Induction*
Owen is very satisfied with the support he gets and describes it as excellent. On one hand, the school really makes an effort to ensure that all new teachers are cared for. There are two weekly meetings with what Owen calls a tutor; this is a group of peers who can support and challenge each other, and they discuss relevant topics. On the other hand, the school also seems to demand a lot. The new teachers are observed several times and have to write essays and reports. Owen describes this as partly good for the feedback and partly keeps him on his toes. The combination of demands and support seems to function well, and Owen seems to put less emphasis on the assessment part. Hargreaves and Goodson (2006) found in a study that the most effective change strategies in schools were exactly to combine both pressure and support; both top-down and bottom up. Owen compares himself with other newly qualified teachers

and criticises the inconsistencies between schools in terms of support. It worries him that teachers without support might not reach their potential (see more about the impact of support in Endre's story).

6   Conclusion

Although Owen enjoys being a teacher and is very satisfied with the support he gets, he is not sure he will stay in education. There are some changes in the educational system that he does not appreciate and is unwilling to be part of. These changes are partly international trends. Interactions have become market-based and performance-driven and the idea of teaching as a broader social mission is undermined. Ballet and Kelchtermans (2009) found in a study that teachers experience they have less time to be creative and to develop collegial relationships. It is changes like these that Owen fears. He is unwilling to teach at any price and to compromise his fundamental values about empowering students. If Owen continues teaching, he sees himself as a leader. He appears to be an ambitious teacher, but he is also a critical thinker.

Note

1   Schools in England which are directly funded by central government and independent of direct control by the local authority.

References

Ballet, K., & Kelchtermans, G. (2009). Struggling with workload: Primary teachers' experience of intensification. *Teaching and Teacher Education, 25*(8), 1150–1157.

Colnerud, G. (2006). Teacher ethics as a research problem: Syntheses achieved and new issues. *Teachers and Teaching: Theory and Practice, 12*(3), 365–385.

Colnerud, G. (2015). Moral stress in teaching practice. *Teachers and Teaching: Theory and Practice, 21*(3), 346–360.

Eisner, E. W. (2002). *The arts and the creation of mind.* New Haven, CT & London: Yale University Press.

Eisner, E. W. (2004). What can education learn from the arts about the practice of education? *International Journal of Education and the Arts, 5*(4), 1–13.

Hargreaves, A., & Goodson, I. (2006). Educational change over time? The sustainability and nonsustainability of three decades of secondary school change and continuity. *Educational Administration Quarterly, 42*(1), 3–41.

Klafki, W. (2002). *Dannelsesteori og didaktik: nye studier*. Århus: Forlaget Klim.

Kyriacou, C., & Kunc, R. (2007). Beginning teachers' expectations of teaching. *Teaching and Teacher Education, 23*, 1246–1257.

Loughran, J. (2010). *What expert teachers do. Enhancing professional knowledge for classroom practice*. New York, NY: Routledge.

Mansfield, C., Beltman, S., & Price, A. (2014). 'I'm coming back again!' The resilience process of early career teachers. *Teachers and Teaching: Theory and Practice, 20*(5), 547–567.

Nussbaum, M. C. (1997). *Cultivating humanity. A classical defense of reform in liberal education*. Cambridge, MA & London: Harvard University Press.

Smith, K., Ulvik, M., & Helleve, I. (2013). *Førstereisen. Lærdom hentet fra nye læreres fortellinger* [First journey – lessons learned from novice teachers]. Oslo: Gyldendal.

Ulvik, M., Smith, K., & Helleve, I. (2009). Novice in secondary school. The coin has two sides. *Teaching and Teacher Education, 25*(6), 835–842.

Young, M. (2013). Overcoming the crisis in curriculum theory: A knowledge based approach. *Journal of Curriculum Studies, 45*(2), 101–118.

PART 3

The Finnish Teacher Education Context

Introduction to Part 3: The Finnish Context

Sven-Erik Hansén

In this brief presentation I will deal with three themes in order to catch some characteristic features in Finnish teacher education. The first will provide a short overview of a few features characterizing teacher education reforms. Focus for the second theme concerns an interpretation of consequences of a choosing a university based approach and finally the third theme will deal with one current ongoing trend, a national mentor-programme for supporting newly qualified teacher (NQTs), will be scrutinized.

Teacher education reform: In the 1970s it shall be Finnish teacher education became transformed to the university, fully integrated in the examination system. A master's degree is required for teacher legitimation, except for pre-school teachers and some branches of teachers for vocational education institutes. Through this transformation all kinds of primary school teacher education was up graded to the same academic level as subject matter teacher education for junior high school and secondary school already had been for about a century.

University based approach: The chosen design means that student teachers practice both teaching and researching during their studies (Välijärvi & Heikkinen, 2012). The process of academization contributed to the status of teachers because a master's degree is well known and acknowledged by the public. Formal requirements for all categories of teachers, except from pre-primary school teacher education (attached to a bachelor's degree) is today 300 ECTS, in practice meaning about five years of fulltime studies. A characteristic feature in Finnish teacher education is a common study unit for all student teachers consisting of 60 ECTS offering a formal general pedagogical qualification. This study unit serves thus as a unifying force between different categories of teachers emphasizing being teacher, or teachership.

The ambition behind the chosen approach is a pronounced research orientation intertwined with a practice orientation in particular practice schools pedagogically subordinated teacher education institution at the universities. As an academic endeavor teacher education is per definition research based. Research is at large central to the function and identity of the university and a Finnish researcher Kansanen (2014), referring to Griffiths (2004) attaches four characteristics; *research-led,* meaning that the study programme is structured according to a systematic analysis of education, *research-oriented,* referring to an integration between teaching and research on teaching, *research-based,* pointing to the ability of pre-service teachers to practice argumentation, decision-making and justification in solving pedagogical problems and *research-informed orientation,* aiming at equipping pre-service teachers with formal research skills. Although the characteristics provide an idealistic view, hardly fully attainable, they offer a clear direction for the aspirations.

Research activities form an obvious explicit part of the programme containing explicit courses in research methods including quantitative and qualitative aspects for student teachers in programmes entirely offered at teacher education departments, like primary school teachers and special education teachers. The qualitatively oriented research of didactics has over time strengthened its position and has thus become the dominating profile.

Within the master-based approach there are paths for qualifying different kinds of teachers. In the teacher education programme for primary schools the main discipline is education (or applied education or general didactics). Beside the main discipline student teachers study school subjects and attached didactics. Furthermore they specialize in one or two school subjects on various levels.

While primary school teachers get both their educational and subject studies at teacher education departments, secondary school teachers are socialized into at different university departments or disciplines with their respective structures, knowledge generation and traditions. Instead of education secondary school student teachers usually take a discipline attached to a school subject as their major subject and one or two minor subjects.

How are the practical parts of teacher education arranged? Teaching practice is manifested in a system of university-based practice schools and to some extent also in field schools. The interactional relation between theory of didactics and teaching practice is apparent along the studies. This relation is important for understanding the idea of a research oriented approach. Student teachers are involved in different aspects of teacher's work through practice and research endeavors. Continuous so-called three-part meetings between teacher educators as researchers, practice school teachers and student teachers enable encounters in various constellations where theory and practice interact.

When looking at teacher education reforms in the Nordic countries during the period since 1960s the occurrence of radical and frequent changes is, except from Finland, an apparent feature. No major reforms of the basic structure have occurred but the prevailing approach enables continuous changes in terms of courses, literature, examination according to decisions made by and approved by the Faculties of education or comparable bodies. Finnish teacher education is internationally considered to have an excellent design, particularly the combination between academic and theoretical studies at the university providing appropriate conditions for practice in particular practice schools subordinated to the Faculties of Education (Hansén, Forsman, Aspfors, & Bendtsen 2012). This fact has obviously contributed to the acknowledge success of Finnish teacher education.

Mentor programmes for NQTs: A national initiative for supporting new teachers in Finland is peer-group mentoring (PGM) was taken in 2010. A special feature is that experienced teachers take a mentor course alongside conducting groups of new teachers. The PGM model has internationally been considered rather unique as it, in relation to several other support programmes, has no elements of assessment, standardization or control. Instead, PGM affords means for both new and experienced teachers to collaborate, reflect and learn together in a supportive environment. As such, the approach is in line with general pedagogical trends in Finland emphasising a high level of teacher autonomy (Aspfors & Hansén, 2011; Heikkinen, Jokinen, & Tynjälä, 2012). PGM has been implemented through a national consortium project called *Osaava Verme*, comprising all the teacher education departments of the universities and vocational teacher education institutions in Finland.[1]

Note

1 For more information see www.osaavaverme.fi

References

Aspfors, J., & Hansén, S.-E. (Eds.). (2011). *Gruppmentorskap som stöd för lärares professionella utveckling*. Helsingfors: Söderströms.

Hansèn, S.-E., Forsman, L., Aspfors, J., & Bendtsen, M. (2012). Visions for teacher education – Experiences from Finland. *Acta Didactica Norway, 1*(6), 1–17.

Heikkinen, H., Jokinen, H., & Tynjälä, P. (Eds.). (2012). *Peer-group mentoring for teacher development*. New York, NY: Routledge.

Kansanen, P. (2014). Teaching as a master's level profession in Finland: Theoretical reflections and practical solutions. In O. MCNamara, J. Murray, & M. Jones (Eds.), *Workplace learning in teacher education. Professional learning and development in schools and higher education* (Vol. 10, pp. 279–292). Dordrecht: Springer.

Välijärvi, J., & Heikkinen, J. (2012). Peer-group mentoring and the culture of teacher education in Finland. In H. Heikkinen, H. Jokinen, & P. Tynjälä (Eds.), *Peer-group mentoring for teacher development* (pp. 31–40). London: Routledge.

CHAPTER 6

Alice's Story: I Cannot Save Everybody

Nobody in my family is a teacher. I think I first thought of becoming a teacher when I attended lower secondary school; in seventh, eighth or ninth grade. When I had finished upper secondary school, I had not yet thought of anything else than becoming a teacher. And I still like children and I enjoy teaching.

It is difficult to become a student teacher in Finland; particularly in the Swedish speaking part of the country. There is only one possible institution and consequently all Swedish-speaking student teachers apply for that institution. I did not succeed the first year so I took one year in Sweden and the next year I entered Finnish teacher education. Of course your grades decide if you can become a student teacher or not, additionally you have to write an essay to prove that you know the Swedish language, and there is also an interview. The other parts were no problem, but I was anxious for the interview. I think that was the worst part of it. But I succeeded.

Now I have worked in a primary school for 1½ years in a school with 200 pupils and approximately 20 teachers. I am a teacher for a 6th grade and I teach all the subjects except gymnastics, music and woodwork. I do not teach religion and geography because I have left those subjects to other teachers, so I teach mathematics, Swedish, Finnish, English, history, physics, chemistry and social studies. I have been a teacher for three semesters and they have been very different for me.

1 The First Semester

The first six months I was very anxious and nervous and actually I do not remember so much from those months. I felt like I was not quite able to follow up. The children had changed teachers every year. They were very talkative. There were many conflicts going on so I think the first six months I did 30% teaching and 70% upbringing and comfort. Looking back I think I did very little teaching. To be honest I remember very little from my first semester. What I remember most is the problems between the girls that I had to handle. There was also serious problems between boys and girls; boys who were bullying. In the beginning I did not understand how serious it actually was. I tried to talk with them, but it did not help. But the more I worked on it the more I understood that the situations could be characterized as bullying. So I talked with my colleagues and asked what I should do and they told me I could take it to the "Bullying-team". I reported it there and they took hold of the pupils who were involved. Then I dropped out and left it to them except for being informed. The "Bullying-team" consists of a sample of selected teachers the public health nurse and maybe some social workers are there as well. I wrote and told about the case and then they cleared up the case. The team also contacts the parents if it is necessary.

2 The Second Semester

I felt more comfortable. I had more time for teaching. I think the main reason was me. One reason was that I felt more calm and confident because I knew the routines. Another reason was that I succeeded in making the class nicer and that there was less noise and trouble. Particularly I remember an incident with one of the boys who had a tremendous anger. He became terribly angry, turned over the chairs, ran out of the door and was impossible to communicate with. Before I entered the class I was told that he normally became very angry, that he turned chairs and tables upside down, ran out and slammed the door. I was also told that there was nothing to do about it. This semester I decided to talk to him about it. We sat down and I asked him: "Can you feel anywhere in your body that you are going to become angry?" And he answered: "Yes, I always get a headache before I become angry". And I said: "Aha! Then perhaps we can make a deal?" So we made a plan that he should point to his head and that was the sign that should tell me to leave him alone. And if he felt that he was unable to take command of himself he should leave the room and sit in the corridor until he felt calm or we had a break and we could talk about what had happened. The problem was that when he became so angry, it was impossible to talk to him, but when he became calm it was very easy. We made a real appointment and I wrote it down on a sheet of paper that I gave to him where it said exactly what we were going to do, and we signed it. And believe me or not ... after that discussion it never happened again. He has neither become angry nor pointed to his head. This was an incident that helped me and him and also the rest of the class, because when he became so angry he disturbed the whole class. I feel that that incident was a key to a new understanding of my own role as a teacher.

3 The Third Semester

The next semester I continued with the same class and this semester was tough again. I felt I had too much work and too much responsibility. I think I pitched my demands to myself too high. Simultaneously, I though the pupils were becoming more and more annoying. One particular problem was another boy in the class who doesn't want to learn anything. He is not angry. He simply doesn't want to work. I think his father is part of the problem since he tells that he did not like school either when he was a boy. In his opinion the boy should not have any home-work. But of course he must have home-work when he does not do anything at school. He was very happy when he had a break and when he was outside. But when he was in the classroom I had to stand beside him all the time if he should do anything. I have talked with different persons about it, like the teachers of special classes and the team who works with adapted education and I think I have done all I could. I have done everything and have to learn that there was no more I can do. The "Verme"-group (Osaava Verme) has helped me to understand that you cannot save everybody. If you have given all you have then you cannot do anything more. Maybe others could have saved him, but not me. But it has been difficult. Finally, I thought the whole class became more and more difficult before I understood that a lot depended on me. I was tired and irritated and scolded the pupils. They did not even have done anything wrong because I had so short temper. Finally, I realized that I needed help. I was stressed. Maybe it is typical for newly qualified teachers, but I never felt that now I am finished and satisfied. I got the diagnosis "heavy depression". I was not on sick-leave, but I took some medicine and now I feel much better.

4 Support

In the mentor-group we are five novice teachers and one mentor. The mentor has long experience and has been educated for Osaava Verme. There are three from my school and two from other schools. We meet once a month and that has been a very good experience for me. Through the network I have realized that being a teacher is my job. I have understood that when I go home I am not supposed to think of it any more. Then I should have my leisure time. And, as I told about the boy in my class: I cannot save everybody. In the group we have discussed different topics like assessment and children with special needs. What are the procedures when the pupils needs more help? Who should we contact inside school and what about the parents?

5 The Fourth Semester

It took me 1½ years to be sure that I wanted to be a teacher. I thought I would feel it earlier. During my studies I thought I would work with the smaller children, but during my first year as a teacher I had gym with 1st and 2nd class and understood that: "No, I will not work with this age-group". They were everywhere and did not listen to me at all. So I realized that I want to teach older children. When I came back this semester and had energy and was glad and laughed with them I understood the importance of how I behave and react myself. If I walk around for one month and am irritated and tired then of course the class will be restless. Looking forward I think the rest of the semester is going to be very exciting. My pupils are in the sixth grade and are going to change school next year. Some of them are nervous and anxious and there is a lot that is going to be sorted before they leave. And I do not know about everything. So I look forward to a busy spring where I have a lot to do. I hope I will be flexible and even though I don't hope so I think it is going to be very hectic. Looking back to the beginning of my career I can see that I am more relaxed concerning the plans I make, but also when I am together with the pupils.

6   What Can We Learn from Alice's Story?

We have chosen to divide Alice's story into four parts. Alice made clear distinctions because the four semesters appeared very differently for her. It is like a movement of waves. Like many other teachers in this book her first semester could be characterized as chaotic. The next one is much better. She experiences a critical incident that makes her more confident and sure that she can manage as a teacher. Anyway, the third semester is a trip down again, due to her feeling of insufficiency before she in the beginning of the forth semester is more optimistic. Day (2007) found that it takes into three years for a teacher to get to know and to feel confident in the profession. Alice has yet only walked half the distance.

6.1   *The Chaotic Beginning*
Common for many of the teachers in this book is that the first semester is a chaotic period, and Alice is no exception. In addition to requirements of being able to teach new classes, the whole context is un-known for the newcomer. During this period they lack all the information that the other teachers have. Who are all these people, what are the daily routines, where do I find the material, who can I ask, what is required from me? Newly qualified teachers have to ask about small, yet important things, problems that could have been avoided if they were provided with practical information from the beginning (Ulvik, Smith, & Helleve, 2009; Ulvik, Smith, & Helleve, 2013). What Alice remembers best from this period is all the problem-solving concerning bullying she had to

handle with the girls in her class. She did not know that the school had a special team to take care of that kind of problems. She tried to solve the problems herself without understanding how serious it actually was. She estimates that without succeeding she spent 70% of her time trying to solve the problems. Finally, when she told her colleagues about it, she understood that this was a kind of problem she could leave to others.

6.2   A Critical Incident

The second semester is remembered as a good period for Alice. When she came back after Christmas she felt that she knew the routines in her school. She also felt that she succeeded better with her class. Like for example Eric from Australia in this book, she mentions one episode that made a great impression on her, that she remembers very well and that gave her a new understanding of herself as a teacher. One of the boys in her class had a tremendous anger. He seemed to be able to turn the classroom upside down, and was impossible to communicate with when he got his temper tantrum. Apparently, his behavior has caused a lot of problems for himself, for his classmates and for the teacher. What Alice did was to sit down beside him, when he was calm and in good moods. She asked him if he got any signs before the thunderstorm of anger burst out. Maybe nobody else had done this before. However, he turned out to be fully aware of what happened in his body and he was able to tell Alice that he got a headache before he became angry. Alice took the boy seriously and even made a written agreement with him saying that whenever he felt the headache coming, he should point to his head and walk out of the room. The funny thing was that it never happened again that he got angry. Tripp (1994) suggests that the term 'critical incident' may have derived from biography in that it refers to some event or situation that marks a significant turning point or change in the life of the subject. These incidents may not be dramatic or obvious. A critical incident is an interpretation of the significance of an event and has been regularly, deeply and extensively reflected upon (unsystematically) (Tipp, 1993, p. 24). According to Woods (1993) critical incidents are "unplanned, unanticipated and uncontrolled. They are flash-points that illuminate in an electrifying instant some key problematic aspect of the teacher's role and which contain, in the same instant, the solution" (Woods, 1993, p. 357). In relation to schools and teachers' careers, critical incidents may be "highly charged moments and episodes that have enormous consequences for personal change and development" (Sikes, Measor, & Woods, 1985, p. 230). Alice says that she feels that the episode with the angry boy has changed her understanding of herself as a teacher.

6.3 *You Cannot Save Everybody*

In the literature "the practice shock" (Flores, 2006) relates to the discrepancy between an ideal perception of teaching and the reality teachers often experience in an early career phase; the mismatch that exists between the idealistic expectations of the professional reality (Achinstein, 2006, p. 123). During a previous life as pupils and student teachers, the "apprenticeship of observation" (Lortie, 1975) novice teachers have developed ideals of education. The conflict may lead to a continual and sometimes conflicting process of challenging personal beliefs, and consequently, of relearning from practice and/or "unlearning". New teachers have to develop a set of coping strategies, according to a survival orientation, to adapt to the new tasks and roles required of them as teachers (Flores, 2006; Kyriacou & Kunc, 2007; Smethem, 2007). The third semester was a tough time for Alice. There may be other reasons for her depression as well, but the fact that she has to admit that she is not able to help all the pupils in her class is a bitter pill to swallow. It hurts her to see that one of the boys, probably a clever boy, does not do his homework and is not willing to do it. The boy's attitude is even supported by his father who thinks that homework is not necessary. For Alice this attitude is unbelievable, but finally she has to accept that she has lost the battle. Le Maistre and Pare (2010) claim that student teachers should be made aware that as future teachers they have to accept solutions that are not always optimal or perfect. Newly qualified teachers, often the best qualified, have high ambitions and blame themselves if they are not able to obtain the best results. The concept "satisficing" refers to the fact that a solution must suffice; it must be sufficient to meet the requirements of the situation, but it must also satisfy the problem solver. Since the sufficient solution is not necessarily the optimal solution, the problem solver must be able to live with a solution that is not perfect (Simon, 1957; Maistre & Pare, 2010, p. 562). Alice became ill. She was irritated, tired, worn out and stressed and realized that she needed help. Finally, she came to the conclusion that she is not able to save everybody if she is going to survive and save herself.

7 Conclusion

By the time of our interview Alice is optimistic. She says that it has taken her 1½ years to make sure that she wants to become a teacher, and she has given us a good illustration of the ups-and-downs she has experienced during this period. Apparently, she has learned a lot about herself as a human being through these three semesters. The fact that new teachers judge their own success on pupils' progress makes them extra vulnerable. Personal engagement means that the borders between personal and professional needs are blurred. When something goes wrong the closest interpretation is to blame yourself as a teacher (Helleve, 2010). Hopefully, Alice has learned her lesson about this kind of distinction.

References

Achinstein, B. (2006). New teacher and mentor political literacy: Reading, navigating and transforming induction contexts. *Teachers and Teaching: Theory and Practice, 12*(2), 123–138.
Flores, M. A. (2006). Being a novice teacher in two different settings: Struggles, continuities, and discontinuities. *Teachers College Record, 108*(10), 2021–2052.
Flores, M. A., & Day, C. (2006). Contexts which shape and reshape new teachers' identities: A multi-perspective study. *Teaching and Teacher Education, 22*(2), 219–232.
Fuller, F. F., & O. H. Brown (1975). Becoming a teacher. In K. Ryan (Ed.), *Teacher Education, the 74th yearbook of the National Society for the study of education.* Chicago, IL: University of Chicago Press.
Helleve, I. (2010). Theoretical foundations of teachers' professional development. In J. Lindberg & A. Olofsson (Eds.), *Online learning Communities and Teacher professional Development. Methods for improved education delivery* (pp. 1–20). Hershey, PA: Information Science Reference.
Kyriacou, C., & Kunc, R. (2007). Beginning teachers' expectations of teaching. *Teaching and Teacher Education, 23*(8), 1246–1257.
Le Maistre, C., & Pare, A. (2010). Whatever it takes: How beginning teachers learn to survive. *Teaching and Teacher Education, 26*, 559–564.
Simon, H. A. (1957). *Models of social and rational.* New York, NY: Wiley.
Sikes, P. J., Measor, L., & Woods, P. (1985). *Teacher careers: Crises and continuities.* Oxford: Taylor & Francis.
Tripp, D. (1993). *Critical Incidents in teaching.* New York, NY: Routledge.
Tripp, D. (1994). Teachers' lives, critical incidents, and professional practice. *Qualitative Studies in Education, 7*(1), 65–76.
Woods, P. (1993). Critical events in education. *British Journal of Sociology of Education, 14*(4), 355–371.

CHAPTER 7

Maria's Story: I Have to Practice What I Preach

I have studied in Vasa to become a general teacher. That means that I have no subject connection. I have studied mathematics as an extra subject, but that is far from the subjects I teach currently. In Finland it is normal for most teachers to teach many different subjects.

Now I work in a small city in a lower secondary and an upper secondary school in combination. I teach health education and gymnastics. I am a substitute teacher until next winter. Actually I am a substitute teacher for a friend of mine who is on maternity leave. It suits me well because now I am at home in the place where I grew up.

I have often wondered why I chose to become a teacher. None of my parents are teachers so that is not the reason. Actually, I have always thought that it must be fun to teach and that it would be a nice profession. I thought it would represent some kind of challenges to help children and young people to understand how important education is. For me it has always been an alternative, but the decision came gradually. However, my mother told me that when we were playing as kids I always acted as a teacher for my younger sisters who were my pupils. Teaching is highly valued in Finland. The profession has high status and it may be difficult to get a job.

Looking back at the first year it has been challenging and interesting and I have learned a lot. I have experienced many situations that I could never had read about in books or learned from exams. I have really understood that every pupil is unique and has his or her own style and personal way of learning. You really have to see every pupil and understand that they learn differently.

What I enjoy most is what I get in return from the pupils. Their success is my success. It gives me a lot. Of course I can be tired and irritated some times, but when I succeed; when I can see that they understand what I have tried to tell them for weeks then I get my reward.

1   The Ethical Challenge

Respect is a key-word for me. An example of what I mean is the 15 year old boys who every day enter the classroom with their caps on. I tell them daily: "Please take off your caps before you come in". Sooner or later you realize that now you have gained respect and they take off their caps before they enter. It is a small detail, but everything starts with the entrance of the classroom. I think that has influenced me as a teacher; the growing respect I feel I have gained. It is like you and the pupil find each other and the ties become stronger and stronger. This means that as a teacher I can give them more and more freedom, loosen the strings in a way. For example there is a boy who initially opposed to all I said. Every time I had a suggestion to a learning activity he had a question. Today he listens, watches and believes what I say. It is important for me that they understand that they learn for their own sake and not for mine. They have to adopt the knowledge and use it themselves. In gymnastics they have to understand that maybe it is better to ride the bike to school instead of being driven in a car by their mother or father. And maybe if they meet a friend it is better to play outside than to watch TV-series the whole evening.

If the pupils are going to believe in me and trust in me then I have to practice what I preach. Consequently, I always ride my bike to school. If I should come to school in a car every day and they always saw me driving I think they would believe that the importance of using a bike is just something she is preaching. She doesn't actually mean what she says. However, to live in a small community can make the combination of private and professional life a bit complicated. In our community there are 12.000 inhabitants so the possibility for meeting some of your pupils in the spare-time is fairly high. The most difficult has perhaps been to be on the same handball-team as some of the oldest pupils in upper secondary school. I also become angry an disappointed when we lose a game like they do, but I feel I have to control myself more than the others who are my pupils.

2 Support

I think the support I have got through the mentorship through Osaava Verme has been very important. Once a month we meet newly qualified teachers from other schools and it has been so important for me! We are four teachers from my school; two from secondary and two from primary school. We are from different schools of different size and different age groups. However, it is nice to hear that all of them have the same kind of challenges either the pupils are 7 or 17. So far we have discussed how to practice the conversation we have to have with every pupil. How to deal with different kinds of problems like bullying or whatever challenges there may be in school or at home. How do you speak to the pupil? We have also discussed how to document if something unusual happens. Another topic that has been discussed is the limits between private and professional. Everybody has her turn to choose what should be discussed on that specific meeting. We have also had case-discussions with different kinds of challenges and how we would have solved the problems in our classrooms. In school I was given a mentor who has helped me with all the practicalities, like for example showing me around the school. We are six-seven newly qualified teachers here. The principle has had three meetings with the group so far. In these meetings we have discussed current issues like if we are comfortable in our job and information about different forthcoming projects in school. So I can ask my mentor or I can ask my principle. She is very open-minded. What has surprised me most of all are my colleagues. They come here every day with lots of humor, and they leave in the same optimistic manner when the day is over. They are taking care of the pupils very professionally. The atmosphere is very pleasant and for me that was a big surprise. My impression is that everybody enjoys being here.

3   The Autonomous Teacher

What I have learned most of all is to be open-minded. I have understood that if you dare to speak to your colleagues about whatever you may wonder about like class-room management, learning-activities or individual pupils there is always somebody that can discuss with you and help you. We have no fixed time on the time-table where everybody has to be present except for the conference every other week where all the teachers are gathered. I decide myself if I stay at school or go home as long as I plan for and teach my pupils. There is of course a common curriculum for Finland, where all schools' plans are collected, but there are no national tests that many countries have. As a teacher I chose the subject matter I want and how I want to adapt it to the single pupil. Actually, there are not so many things that have changed since I was a pupil myself. Of course there are more technical device like Smartboards and films that you can use in computer-rooms. We have two different computer-rooms that we can book. There you find portable PC's, Chromebooks, and different device that you can bring to your classroom if you want to. If I decide beforehand I can also ask my pupils to bring their own telephones to school. I think it is nice that things improve inside schools and not only outside.

4   Outside the Classroom

What I don't like is all the extra assignments I have to do that are not connected to the teaching. I mean extra things that happen like sport-days, guest-lectures or anything else that disturbs my plans for the lessons and steals the time. I do not speak about the documentation I have to do every day. I think that is a piece of cake when you have learned it. We have a digital programme where I write down everything from absence, remarks concerning bad behavior, missing homework, positive feedback from pupils and what kind of topics we have been through every day. The parents can log into the same programme and check their own child if they want to. Of course it was demanding to find out what to write in the beginning, but now I know the system and I think it is good. Eduaction for pupils with special needs works very well in our school. That means that pupils who need it can go to small classes with extra equipment. As a general rule their education does not require more documentation than the other pupils. I think the next semester is going to be very interesting! So many nice things happen in spring. Ninth grade is going to have their grades and new pupils will arrive that are going to be our pupils for next year. These are common events including the entire school society; pupils as well as teachers. We have a common end-of-term with concerts and open house and things like that. A lot of fun is going to take place here now!

5 What Can We Learn from Maria's Story?

5.1 *An Autonomous Profession*
Unlike many other teachers in this book the Finnish teachers, Alice and Maria have not chosen to become teachers because they were born into a family of teachers or because they dreamt about taking care of others since childhood. It is difficult to become a teacher in Finland. Alice and Maria have chosen a profession that has high status in society. One important feature in the Finnish context is that teachers have an important and respected role, comparable to the status of a lawyer or physician. For this reason, the teaching profession is a popular career choice, and the number of applicants in teacher education is high (Sahlberg, 2011). Universities can select students based on academic skills and motivation, students who in turn achieve good outcomes, a process that has been described as a "positive circle of recognition" (Heikkinen & Huttunen, 2004). Finnish teachers have a high degree of autonomy. Maria tells about a school without many meetings and without national tests. What annoys her are not the demands for documentation and accountability, but the fact that events like sports-days and guest-lectures take the pupils' attention away from learning activities in the classroom.

5.2 *Peer-Group Mentoring*
However, the transition from education to teaching is a huge step, also in Finland. In line with Alice, Maria appreciates the possibility she has for

mentorship through what she calls Osaava Verme; peer group mentoring. Peer-group mentoring is a model designed to support the professional development of newly qualified teachers (Helleve & Ulvik, 2011). The model is based on a socio-constructive perspective on learning, valuing dialogue and sharing of knowledge (Geeraerts, Tynjälä, Heikkinen, Markkanen, Pennanen, & Gijbels, 2015). The authors make a distinction between peer-learning and what they call traditional mentoring. Traditional mentoring refers to mentoring models where a more experienced colleague transmits knowledge to the newcomer. While the traditional model is hierarchical, peer-group mentoring is based on the idea that the participants are autonomous equals who share knowledge and learn from each-other. According to the researchers this model suits the policy that promotes the autonomous teacher like the Finnish model does. Maria describes how her group of five teachers from different schools meets every month and how important it is for her to listen to and discuss common challenges.

5.3 *To Teach What You Preach*

Maria is deeply concerned with her own moral behavior as a model for the pupils. Respect is a key-word for her; mutual respect in the sense that if she treats her pupils respectfully they will learn from it and do the same. She believes and experiences that she gradually gains confidence as a teacher. An important reason for teachers to pay attention to their own moral conduct is *respect for the other*; another is being a *role model*, hoping to inspire students by their way of being (Ulvik, Smith, & Helleve, 2017). Patiently, she tells the boys: "Please take off your caps before you come in" every day. She repeats this sentence until at some moment she notices that the headdress has disappeared before they enter the classroom. How teachers act in the classroom reflects value priorities (Colnerud, 2006). According to Løgstrup (1969) you should be aware of the fact that you never communicate with another person without having a piece of the other person's faith in your hands. In a crowded classroom it can be difficult. Maria has a boy in the class who initially opposed to all she said. She meets him with respect and answers his questions and gradually he becomes confident and willing to listen to her. In schools, ethical decisions that require reflection often have to be taken immediately. Improvisation and instant action, without time for reflection is required in what Donald Schön (1987) calls reflection in action. Then it is easy to set aside "the niceties of ethical theory" (Bullough, 2014, p. 252). Teaching at its best acquires artistry, and with in-flight actions, what is to be done has to be felt (Ulvik et al., 2017; Eisner, 2002). Also outside the classroom Maria is concerned with the responsibility she has a model for her pupils. She rides a bike to school every day. Dealing with other people means to hold some part of their lives in our hands, in particular, dealing with vulnerable young people puts an extra responsibility on teachers to be aware of their power. Maria is aware of this responsibility. She is concerned with her obligation and says: "If they are going to believe in me I have to practice what I preach".

6 Conclusion

Maria is optimistic and thinks the next semester is going to be exciting. She enjoys the profession as a teacher. She seems to have been working systematically from the beginning with the aim of gaining respect and she has succeeded.

References

Bullough, R. V. (2014). The way of openness: Moral sphere theory, education, ethics, and classroom management. *Teachers and Teaching: Theory and Practice, 20*(3), 251–263.

Colnerud, G. (2006). Teacher ethics as a research problem: Syntheses achieved and new issues. *Teachers and Teaching: Theory and Practice, 12*(3), 365–385.

Eisner, E. (2002). From episteme to phronesis to artistry in the study and improvement of teaching. *Teaching and Teacher Education, 18*, 375–385.

Geeraerts, K., Tynjälä, P., Heikkinen, H., Markkanen, I., Pennanen, M., & Gijbels, D. (2015). Peer-group mentoring as a tool for teacher development. *European Journal of Teacher Education, 38*(3), 358–377.

Heikkinen, H., & Huttunen, R. (2004). Teaching and the dialectic of recognition. *Pedagogy, Culture and Society, 12*(2), 163–173.

Helleve, I. (2017). Formally educated mentors in Norway. Possibilities and challenges in mentors' support of colleagues' professional development. *Nordvei, 2*(1), 30–44.

Helleve, I., & Ulvik, M. (2011). Is individual mentoring the only answer? *Education Inquiry, 2*(1), 123–135.

Levinas, E. (1979). *Totality and infinity: An essay on exteriority.* London: Kluwer Academic Publishers.

Løgstrup, K. E. (1969/2000). *Den etiske fordring* [The ethical demand]. Oslo: Cappelen.

Sahlberg, P. (2011). *Finnish lessons. What can the world learn from educational change in Finland?* New York, NY: Teachers College Press.

Schön, D. (1987). *Educating the reflective practitioner.* San Francisco, CA: Jossey-Bass.

Silander, T., & Välijärvi, J. (2013). The theory and practice of building pedagogical skill in Finnish teacher education. In H.-D. Meyer & A. Benavot (Eds.), *PISA, power and policy. The emergence of global educational governance* (pp. 77–97). Oxford: Symposium Books.

Tynjälä, P. (2008). Perspectives into learning at the workplace. *Educational Research Review, 3*(2), 130–154.

Ulvik, M., Smith, K., & Helleve, I. (2017). Ethical aspects of dilemmas in the first year of teaching. *Professional Development in Teaching, 43*(2), 236–252.

PART 4

The Israeli Teacher Education Context

Introduction to Part 4: The Israeli Context

Lily Orland-Barak

Like many other countries, the education of teachers in Israel is regarded as core to the development of society, despite the huge gap between this ideal vision of teachers and teaching and teachers' low professional status when compared to other professions. In this paradoxical positioning, along with recurrent public criticism regarding teachers' lack of competence and preparation for bringing students to higher levels of achievement in comparative international tests (Ariav & Kfir, 2008), teacher education policy devotes substantial attention to problems related to the selection, preparation and support of quality teachers and teaching. Teacher education programmes in colleges are also criticized for being too permissive in their acceptance criteria and not rigorous enough in their selection and qualification processes.

The expansion of Israeli higher education, in the early 1990's, brought to a growing funding (OECD, 2006) that was directed and distributed by the parliament's 'Committee for Planning and Budgeting' (CPB, 1996). The funding model for resources' distribution amongst higher education institutions is based on two components: Research (46%) and teaching (54%) (Council for Higher Education, 2006a, 2006b), to the exclusion of clinical experience as integral to professional higher education studies. Along with forces pushing higher education towards basic research and applied knowledge models, there is a widespread acknowledgement of the added value of creating meaningful connections between schools and universities (BERA-RSA, 2014; Sorensen, Twidle, & Childs, 2014; Zeichner, 2010).

Israeli teacher education is governed by two public institutions: The Ministry of Education and The Council for Higher Education. The Ministry of Education is in charge of planning and budgeting teacher education programmes in colleges. The Council of Higher Education is responsible for approving academic qualification programmes and degrees. The active involvement of these two bodies is demonstrated in several core policy documents, reports and reforms that have had major implications on the orientation of teacher education in Israel. Among these documents are the Ben-Peretz commission (Ministry of Education, 2001) and The Dovrat Commission (National Task Force for the Advancement of Education in Israel, 2005) initiated by the Ministry of Education; and the Teacher Training Guidelines (1981) and The Ariav Committee Report, invited by the Council of Higher Education (2006b). A new committee for re-thinking guidelines for teacher education in the 21st century was recently appointed and is now working on a new set of guidelines. The outcome of the above processes over the years has been the increase of teacher education programmes offered in the market (too many at the moment) and, at the same time, the promotion of academization processes that require the integration of academic and subject matter contents into the teacher education curriculum. Recently, and influenced by worldwide trends, there has also been a strong movement towards integrating contents related to workplace learning, creating synergies and meaningful links between student teachers' learning at the academic institutions and mentored learning at the workplace (Maskit & Orland-Barak, 2015).

In general, extant Israeli policy regarding teacher education curricula adopts a vision of the teacher as a clinician. This type of teacher would be skillful in diagnosing pupils' learning abilities and styles, adjusting the curriculum accordingly and evaluating behaviors to align with learning outcomes (Beck, 2013). Israeli Teacher Education incorporates two main models of practice teaching: The traditional apprenticeship model, in which the student teacher functions as a protégé of an experienced teacher in school, occasionally teaching lessons or parts of them; and the professional development model (PDS) around partnerships created between the university/colleges and the schools with mentors both from the school and the university (Lahavy, 2009). The majority of teachers are initially qualified in education colleges, whereas universities grant only high-school teaching diplomas (Hoffman & Niederland, 2012).

References

Ariav, T., & Kfir, D. (2008). The teacher training crisis: Characteristics and suggestions for improvement. In T. Ariav & D. Kfir (Eds.), *The teaching crisis: Towards a reformed teacher training* (pp. 335–346). Jerusalem: Van Leer Institute. [in Hebrew]

Beck, S. (2013). The changing face of teacher education in Israeli colleges. In S. Shimony (Ed.), *On the continuity line: Training, specialization and teachers' professional development – Policy, theory and practice* (pp. 60–92). Tel Aviv: Mofet/Ministry of Education. [in Hebrew]

British Educational Research Association. (2014). *Research and the teaching profession: Building the capacity for a self-improving education system* (Final Report of the BERA-RSA Inquiry into the Role of Research in Teacher Education). London: BERA.

Committee for Planning and Budgeting Committee. (1996). Position paper for the public committee of tuition policy in higher education institutions. In *A report by the public committee of tuition policy and aid projects for students in higher education institutions, 1991–1196* (Chaired by Supreme Court judge (retired)). Yaacob Meletz. [in Hebrew]

Council for Higher Education. (1981) *Degem manche letochnit limudim letoar boger behora'a* [Guidelines for a Curriculum for a Bachelor of Education Degree]. Jerusalem: Council for Higher Education. [in Hebrew]

Council of Higher Education. (2006a). *Higher education council report 2004–2005, No. 31/32*. Jerusalem: Council for Higher Education. [in Hebrew]

Council for Higher Education. (2006b) *Doch hava'ada likviat mitvim manchim laachshara lehora'a bamosadot lehaskala gevoha beisrael* [Report of the Committee for Determining Outlines for Teacher Training in Higher Education Institutions in Israel] (The Ariav Report). Jerusalem: Council for Higher Education. [in Hebrew]

Hoffman, A., & Niederland, D. (2012). Is teacher education higher education? The politics of teacher education in Israel, 1970–2010. *Higher Education Policy, 25*, 87–106.

Lahavy, Y. (2009). "Hands first": On practical experience in teacher education. *Hed Ha'chinuch, 84*(3), 62–64. [in Hebrew]

Maskit, D., & Orland-Barak, L. (2015). University–school partnerships: Student teachers' evaluations across nine partnerships in Israel. *Journal of Education for Teaching, 41*(3), 285–306.

Ministry of Education. (2001) *Hachsharat morim beisrael bitemurot hazman* [Teacher Training in Israel over the Course of Time] (Report of the Ben Peretz Commission). Jerusalem: Ministry of Education. [in Hebrew]

National Task Force for the Advancement of Education in Israel [Dovrat Commission]. (January, 2005). *National Program for Education* [Dovrat Report]. Jerusalem: State of Israel.

OECD. (2006). *Education at a glance*. Retrieved August 16, 2012, from http://www.oecd.org/document/52/0,3343,en_2649_39263238_37328564_1_1_1_1,00.html

Sorensen, P., Twidle, J., & Childs, A. (2014). Collaborative approaches in initial teacher education: lessons from approaches to developing student teachers' use of the Internet in science teaching. *Teacher Development, 18*(1), 107–123.

Zeichner. (2010). Rethinking the connections between campus courses and field experiences in college-and university-based teacher education. *Journal of Teacher Education, 61*(1–2), 89–99.

CHAPTER 8

Aviva's Story: Teaching Is a Call

1   Becoming a Teacher

I am a special education teacher in elementary school. I was educated at the University, majoring in special education, and now I am the homeroom teacher for a small class, 15 students with behavioural and emotional problems. This is my first year of teaching and as a homeroom teacher I have to teach more or less all subjects.

I decided to become a teacher not because of the money, because teachers are not paid very well here in Israel, even if you have a university education. So, if I wanted to become rich, teaching would not be a good job. I wanted to become a teacher because of idealism in a way, I wanted to help those children who were less fortunate in life to function in the society, yes, I wanted in a way to form the next generation. I really understood the importance of education, not only for the children themselves, but also for our future society. You can, sort of, say that I chose teaching out of idealism, which is, perhaps, not very cool these days. Anyhow, I studied what I wanted and now I have a job that I aspired to have as well.

2   Challenges and Rewards

The year started off really bad. It was very, very difficult, especially because my expectations of how to help children were much tougher to fulfill than I had foreseen. There were smaller things I had never thought of would be my job, such as making sure the kids had eaten, or even help some of them get dressed or put on their shoes. But there were also more difficult challenges when I saw that a child really suffered in school, or that parents were quarreling in front of me at parent meetings, and each one wanted support from me when 'fighting' over what was best for their child. Theories about education and special education had not prepared me for these situations, and the famous, or notorious theory–practice gap was right there, straight in my face.

The situation improved, though, slowly, but surely, and I suppose time was the best medicine. I learned and learned, reflected and reflected, revisited my understandings and beliefs time and again, and I grew. I felt the students did the same, and it was like we were growing together, like learning to be with each other, to spend a great deal of our time together. I especially felt how smoother our relationship had become and how I had started to enjoy teaching and being with these kids in the middle of the second semester, around Passover. Passover is a long vacation during which I started to miss school and my students even though the holiday was filled with family visits and trips, so it was not a question of being bored, it was something more, deeper in a way. When I came to school after the vacation I was so pleased to hear the kids say they had missed me to, and that in the next vacation they wanted us to meet. "During the vacation we don't know what to do, it is sometimes boring. In school we do fun things", one of my students said when school started after Passover. That really made me happy.

Sometimes I ask myself what I like about teaching, and the answer seems to be that what I like most is to see that I influence students' knowledge development, what I teach and what we talk about in class makes the world richer and bigger for these kids. That is a good feeling. I also think that I have an impact on the way they see the world, on what is right and wrong, and that is sometimes felt as a very heavy responsibility. I am who I am, and this might have an impact on how these kids will look at the world as adults, values, morals and things like that. So I try all the time to do the right things, to say the right things and to discuss moral dilemmas with them like when there is a problem, what are the for and against of the various solutions to the problem. I sometimes question myself if I am a good enough person to take on this heavy responsibility in forming the future of these kids.

3 Critical Incidents

But I do not only have positive experiences from teaching, and a thing that surprised during this first year is that some students, even these young kids, have a negative attitude to teachers, not especially in my class or in special education, but in school in general. The school where I work is not a school for special education students, it has all kinds of students, like most schools, I suppose. Some students behave rather disrespectfully to the teachers, it is the way they talk to them and about them, the way they do not accept or follow instructions, and even behave violently to the teachers. It happened to me when I was being on 'guard' duty in the school yard in one of the breaks, and I had to stop one of the older kids from using his skateboard because it endangered the other students. He pushed me away and threatened to hit me after school with his friends because I behaved 'like the police'. Well, nothing came out of it, I talked to his homeroom teacher and that was that, but the confidence in his threatening behavior towards me really shocked me. At this point I really asked myself if I wanted to stay a teacher and work in this kind of environment, and it was a yes/no question for me. I decided to stay, and to help children pave the way to success and a good life at any cost. But I understood that all the time I had had a little bird in the back of my mind nagging me from time to time saying I did not really want to have this job and I should quit. The turning point was in fact, this unpleasant incident, and I felt good after having taken this decision, and from that point on, it all went much better. I had made the decision to continue teaching.

Another incident which really impressed me was when I saw how a small thing could make a big difference to a student. This little girl had difficulties in getting dressed by herself, and putting on her backpack by herself, was an impossible task. I worked with her for half a year and she could just not get the arm movements right, it was as if the arms had their own mind and moved as they wanted, not wanting to carry the backpack. She strived and failed, and this, seemingly little thing, made her refrain from participating in class, she did not talk in class, and she isolated herself from me and from the other students. Afterwards she said that all she could think of was how she at the end of the day had to struggle with the backpack. She did not give up, however, and neither did I, and when the other kids had left, we practiced for a short while every day. Then, suddenly one day she succeeded in putting on her backpack all by herself, and she took it off and did it again, as if she did not really believe she had done it. She succeeded and had learned how to put on her backpack. This was a major achievement for her. The success changed her completely, she became active in class, talked and took responsibility, and became, in fact, rather dominant. This was an eye opener for me as a teacher, to learn how such minor things become major struggles in a child's life, and how the feeling of success can change a whole person.

4   Support

I found much support during the first year in the mentor whose responsibility it was to induce me into the teaching job. She had done that before, and in our school, and especially when teaching children who need special attention, it was important to have somebody to lean on when things got tough. She helped me through the very difficult times, as when I thought I should leave, and she rejoiced with me when I told her about my successes. She is much older than I am, so I cannot say she became like a friend, but she certainly become like a mother or older sister I could turn to at school. I never had the feeling of being alone, there was always somebody there.

5 Future Plans

I do not know if I will always stay a teacher, but I know that I will probably stay in education, because I have learned that there is no such thing as giving up, and everything is possible if you really put your mind and time to it. It is worthwhile challenging every single student and support him or her finding their optimal speed of progress towards their own goals.

6 What Does Aviva's Story Tell Us?

Aviva's story tells about a warm person who is dedicated to her job and to her students in spite of her choice to work with 'less fortunate students' as she calls them, a special education class. That is what she wanted to do when she started her education as a special education teacher, and it says quite a lot about her motivation for becoming a teacher.

6.1 *Motivation*

In the previous story about Yael, the main motivation for teaching was intrinsic, she wanted to work with her subject. This type of motivation is quite different from the motivation we notice in Aviva's story. Aviva's motivation to be a teacher was, already at the very beginning, altruistic. She became a teacher out of idealism "I wanted to help those children who were less fortunate in life to function in the society, yes, I wanted in a way to form the next generation". This is a strong statement Aviva presents, yet it correspondences well with international research on motivation for teaching, primary school teachers have a strong altruistic and social utility motif for becoming teachers whereas secondary school teachers are more subject oriented (Watt, Richardson, & Smith, 2017). When students of teaching enter the profession with strong altruistic motivation, they are likely to see teaching as 'a call' or a mission. This makes them vulnerable when they realize that in their daily work more formal aspects of the job such as teaching according to a fixed curriculum, demands for documentation, unpleasant meetings with parents, and little autonomy due to long methodological traditions in the school takes all the time. There is no time left for enacting the pedagogy in which they believe (Smith, Ulvik, & Helleve, 2013). They experience, as Aviva said so clearly, the notorious practice shock. It might seem that during her teacher education, Aviva had become familiar with the concept, practice shock, but only in theory, and she was not prepared when she felt it day after day in school. It was related to making sure the children were dressed properly, ate during the day or coping with parents who fought about what was best for their child in front of Aviva, the teacher, and perhaps worse, in front of the child. Research tells us that early burn out as a result of the practice shock plays an important role in novices' decision to leave the profession after a short while (Caspersen & Raaen, 2014; Dicke, Parker, & Holtzberger, 2015). The reality of being a teacher can be very different from the expectations. However, contrary to many other novice teachers, Aviva worked herself through the challenges, by looking into herself, reflecting and growing, as she says above. She stayed firm to her own altruistic beliefs, and she was confident enough to practice teaching in alignment with her own beliefs.

6.2 Rewards and Challenges

As a special education teacher Aviva learned to enjoy achievements which might, at first sight, seem insignificant to many and which cannot be measured by tests. Yet, when Aviva saw how important these small achievements were for the children, they became meaningful to her as well. The anecdote about the little girl who had difficulties putting on her backpack at school influenced the whole school day for her and she isolated herself from the other children and from the teacher. Aviva showed what we chose to call *pedagogical empathy*, which means she recognized the child's feelings, and was able to identify possible causes for it (Keen, 2007). Pedagogical empathy is, as understood in this paper, a combination of two aspects of empathy, an affective and a cognitive aspect (Lockwood, Seara-Cardoso, & Viding, 2014). The affective aspect relates to the sensitivity towards a student's feelings expressing warmth and understanding, whereas the cognitive aspect refers to the extent to which a teacher understands and can act supportively to help the student. Pedagogical empathy requires action. Aviva sensed that something bothered the little girl. She observed how she did not talk to the other children and isolated herself. When starting to look for the reasons for this, she also noticed that leaving school at the end of the day was problematic because of the difficulties with the backpack. The student probably felt embarrassed and developed low self-confidence when comparing herself to her peers. They could all put on their backpacks by themselves. Not to embarrass her, Aviva practiced with the girl after the other children had left and by this she also showed what van Manen (1991, 2016) calls pedagogical tact or pedagogical thoughtfulness. At the end of the day only Aviva and the little girl were able to recognise the greatness of this, which to others would be a rather insignificant achievement.

The way Aviva talks about growing with the students and developing a close emotional relationship with the class strengthens the impression that she truly enacted her philosophy of education and educational beliefs. She does not talk about cognitive achievements of her students, but she describes and finds much satisfaction and energy in the relationship she developed with the class during the first year, illustrated by the mutual longing to meet after the two weeks Passover vacation. Veldman, van Tartwijk, Brekelmans, and Wubbels (2013) found in a case study of four veteran teachers that their job satisfaction was closely related to the perceived relationship they had with the students. It seems to be the same for novice teachers, and in our study we found that relations with the students was a factor in new teachers' decision to stay in the profession (Smith, Ulvik, & Helleve, 2013). Student–teacher relationship is one component in the resilience model discussed in the last chapter of this book.

However, not everything went smoothly in Aviva's first year. She discovered that parents were not always considerate of their child's feelings when they highly disagreed about how to support the child in overcoming the many challenges special education children might have. Being close to and caring for her students, it was difficult for Aviva to accept and to handle such a situation. Neither was she prepared for the disrespect of teachers she observed from some of the main stream students, herself being threatened by one of the students. She really started to doubt if she had chosen the right profession, and as she said, "educational theories had not prepared me for this". Educational theories cannot possibly prepare teachers to be for every situation they will meet in their first year or later on in their teaching career, and neither should they. The main goal of initial teacher education should be to provide teachers-to-be with sufficient background knowledge and skills to survive the first phase of their career. During teacher education they should be supported in developing a strong feeling of self-efficacy (Bandura, 1977) which will help them overcome the challenges by believing that they are able to grow into good teachers and execute professional agency (Biesta, Priestly, & Robinson, 2015). Teachers take control over their own practice and act in a manner which agrees with their professional and pedagogical believes. They are not totally governed by external rules and decisions. Such a form for professionalism is important when teachers have to make on-spot decisions in unexpected and challenging situations. They need to draw on their professional theoretical knowledge, but they also have to be able to analyse and act in a responsible manner, which depends on the situation, and the people involved. Professional teachers lean on their professional wisdom (Smith, 2011). Novice teachers cannot look back at years of experience during which professional wisdom is likely to develop, they will, to a large extent, draw on their motivation to be teachers, knowledge from education, empathetic skills and confidence to enact professional agency. Aviva tells us, in her story, that the resources she draws upon when it gets tough, to a large extent, draw on the above.

6.3 *Support*

Aviva also found support in her dedicated and experienced mentor who was always there for her when things got tough. In creating her personal professional wisdom in the teaching of special education children, she got access to her mentor's wealth of wisdom. She was not alone, but 'led by the hand' as they call mentors in Sweden, through the first difficult yet rewarding year. The importance of mentoring during the first phase of teaching is a central theme in various chapters of the book, and therefore the discussion will be rather brief here. Some of the metaphors that mentor themselves have suggested are sometimes functioning as a GPS and at other times as the Wailing Wall (Smith, 2017). The role you take on as a mentor greatly depends on the context and needs of the mentee, and in our case, the novice teacher (American Coastguard Mentor document[1]).But mentoring in itself is not necessarily useful, it has to be quality mentoring, and not all experienced teachers are able to offer mentoring. Therefore they have to be carefully selected, and it seems as if Aviva was fortunate to have such an experienced and professional mentor.

7 Conclusion

Aviva's story tells about a warm person who has become a dedicated teacher with much love for the children and not only enjoying the act of teaching in itself. She struggles through the first year, as do many novice teachers, but driven by her altruistic motivation and the confidence that she can do something for less fortunate children, she overcomes the challenges. Instead of giving up, Aviva grows because she was able to reflect and respond to the difficulties in what she believed to be right pedagogical ways. She herself practiced what she wanted from her students, "whenever you out your mind to something, you can achieve it". She stayed true to her beliefs and supported by her experienced and available mentor, Aviva is looking forward to next year with optimism and enthusiasm. She is one of those teachers who Watt and Richardson (2008) call highly engaged persisters who are dedicated teachers finding professional satisfaction working with children.

Note

[1] See https://media.defense.gov/2017/Mar/14/2001716254/-1/-1/0/CI_5350_24C.PDF

References

Bandura, A. (1977). Self-efficacy: Toward a unifying theory of behavioral change. *Psychological Review, 84*(2), 191.

Biesta, G., Priestley, M., & Robinson, S. (2015). The role of beliefs in teacher agency. *Teachers and Teaching, 21*(6), 624–640.

Caspersen, J., & Raaen, F. D. (2014). Novice teachers and how they cope. *Teachers and Teaching, 20*(2), 189–211.

Dicke, T., Parker, P. D., Holzberger, D., Kunina-Habenicht, O., Kunter, M., & Leutner, D. (2015). Beginning teachers' efficacy and emotional exhaustion: Latent changes, reciprocity, and the influence of professional knowledge. *Contemporary Educational Psychology, 41*, 62–72.

Keen, S. (2007). *Empathy and the novel.* Oxford: Oxford University Press.

Lockwood, P. L., Seara-Cardoso, A., & Viding, E. (2014). Emotion regulation moderates the association between empathy and prosocial behavior. *PLoS One, 9*(5), e96555. doi:10.1371/journal.pone.0096555

Smith, K. (2011). Professional development of teachers – A prerequisite for AfL to be successfully implemented in the classroom. *Studies in Educational Evaluation, 37*(1), 55–61.

Smith, K. (2017). Mentorrollen—Norske og internasjonale stemmer [The role of the mentor – Norwegian and International Voices]. In K. Smith & M. Ulvik (Eds.), *Veiledning av nye lærere–nasjonale og internasjonale perspektiver* [Mentoring Newly Qualified Teachers–National and International Perspectives] (2nd ed., Chapter 1). Oslo: Universitetsforlaget.

Smith, K., Ulvik, M., & Helleve, I. (2013). *Førstereisen—Lærdom hentet fra nye læreres fortellinger* [The first journey. Lessons learned from newly qualified teachers]. Oslo: Gyldendal Akademisk.

Van Manen, M. (1991). *The tact of teaching: The meaning of pedagogical thoughtfulness.* Albany, NY: SUNY Press.

Van Manen, M. (2016). *Pedagogical tact: Knowing what to do when you don't know what to do* (Vol. 1). New York, NY: Routledge.

Veldman, I., van Tartwijk, J., Brekelmans, M., & Wubbels, T. (2013). Job satisfaction and teacher–student relationships across the teaching career: Four case studies. *Teaching and Teacher Education, 32*, 55–65.

Watt, H. M. G., Richardson, P. J., & Smith, K. (2017). Why teach? How teachers' motivations matter around the world. In H. Watt, P. Richardson, & K. Smith (Eds.), *Global perspectives on teacher motivation* (pp. 1–21). Cambridge: Cambridge University Press.

Watt, H. M. G., & Richardson, P. W. (2008). Motivations, perceptions, and aspirations concerning teaching as a career for different types of beginning teachers. *Learning and Instruction, 18*(5), 408–428.

CHAPTER 9

Yael's Story: Mary Poppins of Geography

1   Motivation

Yael teaches geography in a secondary big urban school in a large town in Israel. She was educated at a Teacher Education College and at the University, so she feels she has a solid education behind me, subject studies as well as teacher education.

I became a teacher first of all because I think it is very important to educate the future generation and second because I love geography, and I believe in the significance of geography and in environmental studies to secure a better world. I think geography and environmental studies provide the students with a breadth of knowledge that stretches far beyond what they have to learn in the curriculum and to pass the exam.

2   Challenges and Rewards

I was very enthusiastic when I started teaching, and this first year has been challenging, definitely, but also rather successful, I would say. The main challenges are related to discipline problems, and to having to 'force' unmotivated students to learn. I did not feel I could do that, how could I change their mind or tell them to be interested in geography when they had completely other things on their mind? This was tough, and there are a lot of students like that. So, if I am to say what I do not like about teaching, then it really is the feeling of being responsible for somebody else's motivation. You do not just press a button, and then the student becomes motivated, you cannot tell somebody to be more motivated. That is hard.

But, on the other hand, the best of teaching is when I can see the spark of interest igniting in the students' eyes, when I really feel that 'Yes, they are with me!' When I can see that they are really interested and find the lessons meaningful I feel that this is all teaching is about. The satisfaction or feeling of success when I have succeeded in awakening their will to learn, to be a teacher is the best job you can have. I think this enlightening is what has impressed me most by being a teacher. I was not aware that the impact a teacher has on students' learning could be so strong. I could really follow the transformation in the students' knowledge. They arrived in the beginning of the year without a clue about geography, they could barely place their own home town on the map. And eight months later, they cannot only place their own and other cities on the map, but they have developed a regional analysis of all aspects of geography, demographic, economic, climate-wise, and I could go on and on. It is fantastic. They are now ready to pass the highest level of the national exams.

One of the most surprising things I have learned as a teacher is that I really am able to do something about the students' motivation to learn geography, and what I find most difficult becomes, when I succeed, the most satisfying thing about teaching. The most 'anti'-student, the one with zero motivation at the beginning of the year can change, and become hardworking and successful if I find the right channel in my communication with him. That is really rewarding, and I think only teachers experience this kind of satisfaction.

3   Critical Incidents

An incident from the first year, which I will always carry with me, took place at the end of the first year. I was given a class consisting mainly of disadvantaged youth. They came from low socio-economic backgrounds, many from one-parent families or split-up families, some were new immigrants and had not found their place in the Israeli society. Those who spoke Hebrew with a strong accent were laughed at, and in their desperate attempts to become like the others, they 'went native', meaning they tried to be even more Israeli than the native Israelis, and were bullied because of that. One of these 'tough' boys stopped coming regularly to class in the middle of the second semester, and I really had to insist that he would continue to come to classes. I talked to him again and again, looked him up in the school yard and said that we missed him, gave him responsibilities for the next lesson (look for something on YouTube, searching for information we needed in the lesson, and things like that). If he did not come, it would change the lesson that the whole class had been involved with in planning. The other students did not like that, and let him know it in their ways. So he started to come to class regularly as he had done before. At the very end of the year when we said our good byes, and I told them that I would not be teaching them the following year, he was agitated and blaming me personally. "You are like Mary Poppins of geography", he said, "you come to us, get us interested in geography, make it fun, and then you just get up and leave. That is not right for a teacher to do". At the same time as I was taken by surprise to hear him talk like that, and really sad that his last sentence to me was full of blame and anger, I became excited and happy. I had really made a difference to this boy, at least in his learning of geography. But it is an emotional burden to leave your students with whom you have established a good relationship, they become, in a way, like your children. I suppose it will happen again and again as a teacher, but I think I will find it tough.

4 Support

During the year I suppose I was lucky, but I feel I was supported by colleagues and even the principal. They all helped me handle discipline problems when I was lost. The main supporter was, however, the mentor I was given on my first day in school. I could talk to her about everything, and there were many outside-teaching things with my students I had to take care of, and I had no idea how to do that. But she helped me, and we talked and talked, and together we always found a solution. She was really good to have all the time.

5 Looking Back

One of the things that I learned from this first year was that whatever happens, the best I can do is to remain calm and clear and persistent. Teachers have to talk to students as equals and not look down at them because they are younger or do not have the same education yet. Another thing which I think is very important is that I have to explain the essence behind what I am doing. I just have to make sure that the students understand the reasons why they are asked to do something, or why I teach the way I do. When I do that, I found that most students become less reluctant to do boring things, they accept it in a way because there is a logic behind it. Many students are really great people, you just have to find the way to them and see through the roles they are supposed to play as 'difficult teenagers'. I really like the students, and it is interesting (and very challenging) to work with them.

When looking back at this first year, I think it was good, all in all. There were many tough times, but I never felt I was really alone, there was always someone to talk to, somebody who would help me. What I have learned most is about the students, I think I understand them better now, and therefore it is easier to stay calm when difficult situations arise, and they always do. I am surprised that I succeeded in staying calm, most of the time, but I tell myself all the time that it is not about me, it is about the students. Then I become more patient.

I really want to continue teaching or to stay in education, and perhaps I will advance in the future, to become a coordinator and perhaps a school principal. But I want to stay in education.

6. What Does Yael's Story Tell Us?

Yael's story is, in many way a typical as well as an atypical story about the first year of teaching. She faced challenges, as most novices do (Ulvik, Smith, & Helleve, 2009). But she managed to handle the challenges in a positive way and turn them to learning experiences, also because of the support she found in the school as a whole, the assigned mentor, the colleagues as well as the principal. Her main rewards were related to the students, and in the feedback they gave her, and in the relationships she developed with some of the most difficult students. It seems that good relationships with students as well as with her colleagues made her more resilient when things became difficult. This aligns with findings in Castro, Kelly, and Shih's (2010) study) who twice interviewed 15 novice teachers in high needs areas asking about strategies and resources used to meet challenges when they occurred. They found, among other things, that turning to the colleagues and the school leadership in addition to the students themselves, helped them to successfully meet and overcome obstacles during the first year. Gu and Day (2007) claim that resilience is found in "social systems of interrelationships" (p. 1305). There are, however, a few other issues we found worthwhile discussing after listening to Yael's story.

6.1 *Motivation*

Yael became a teacher because she wanted to work for a better world by teaching future generations about geography and its importance in taking care of the environment. These are visionary words, but Yael does not differ from other novice teachers in her motivation. She teachers in secondary school and Roness and Smith (2010) found that wanting to work with a subject, and in this case, geography, as well as creating an awareness among students of the importance of that subject were the main motivating factors for becoming teachers in secondary school. This form for internal motivation for teaching, combined with a more social utility type of motivation is not unusual and found in several international studies on motivation for teaching using the same instrument to measure motivation, The factors influencing teaching choice (FIT-choice) scale (Watt et al., 2012). Intrinsic motivation differs, to a large extent, from the more altruistic type of motivation which is more common among primary school teachers and which will be further described in Aviva's story in this book. What is encouraging in Yael's story is that she did not become disillusioned during her first year of teaching, and her strong motivation to become a teacher does not seem to decrease during the first year of her teaching. We have researched new teachers' narratives in Norway, and many novices tell about entering the profession with a strong motivation to make a difference, but when they started teaching the reality left little space for intrinsic and social utility motivation. There were too many accountability requirements for documentation and curriculum demands that they had little time left to teach as they had planned and believed in (Smith, Ulvik, & Helleve, 2013).

6.2 Talking to Students as Equals

Another issue that draws our attention in Yael's story is an illustration of her strong intrinsic motivation for teaching as it comes through in her attitude to her students. She finds it important to "talk to students as equals and not look down on them because they are younger or have less education". Consciously or non-consciously Yael's words is a repetition of the Israeli educational philosopher, Dov Darom's words from 2000 in a paper about humanistic education:

> Humanistic education is based on dialogue. This is the 'I' and 'thou' type of dialogue (Martin Buber) whose lessons is learned as well as practiced. True dialogue can take place only among equals (Paulo Freire, 1973). Looking at this issue superficially, one can come to conclude there is no equality between teachers and pupils. Their knowledge and life experiences can truly not be said to be equal. In their basic humanity, however, in their need to be heard, respected, accepted, never humiliated, there is a large degree of equality; their personal needs, aspirations dreams and hope, strengths and weaknesses are valued equally. If we can address our pupils in this frame of mind, we create the foundation for meaningful educational dialogue. (Darom, 2000, p. 26)

Yael did not choose to be a teacher because she wanted to excise power over other people, but truly to make them interested in her subject, geography which she finds important for ensuring a good future for the coming generations. By respecting her students for who they are and by treating them with respect, she has developed strong relationship with even the most difficult students by showing them that she trusted them and gave them responsibilities on which the whole class depended. Yael tells about how this changed the attitude of one of the most difficult students, a tough case, and a relationship built on mutual trust developed. Furthermore, Yael also had a form for meta-talks with her students when she wanted to involve them in difficult tasks and activities. She explained to them why she did what she did, and why she believed it would be useful for their learning. This is truly treating the students with respect and accepted, and it helped her to create a meaningful dialogue with the students.

6.3 Ending Relationships

However, there was also a price to pay at the end of the year when Yael understood she would not teach the same students next year. She had changed their attitude to geography, they enjoyed it, understood the importance of it, and then she left. As one of her students said: "You are like Mary Poppins of geography, you come to us, get us interested in geography, make it fun, and then you just get up and leave. That is not right for a teacher to do". Yael felt guilty of being the Mary Poppins of georgraphy, but at the same time she also felt rewarded, because she understood she had made an impact on her students, and that is what teaching is all about. But ending good relationship is not easy, not even for teachers who have to do this over and over again in their career. Hargreaves & Tucker argued already in 1991 that research on teachers' feelings had been neglected, and we claim that the situation is not much different today. Hargreaves (2000) also writes about the positive and negative effect of relationships with students and in his study of 53 teachers he found that it is more difficult for secondary school teachers to develop good relationships with their students than is the case for primary school teachers. However, when this is done, as in Yael's case, it is also harder to end the relationship at the end of the school year. This can be an emotional burden for teachers. Yael does not talk about this as an emotional strain, she feels guilty, yet rewarded. It becomes a question of learning from the positive experiences, yet being able to look forward and prepare for new classes, new students and new challenges. Yael seems to be able to do so.

7 Conclusion

Yael's story is a positive narrative about the first year as teacher. She was highly motivated to start teaching and the motivation is still there after the first year, even though it was challenging. She was strongly supported, not only by the assigned mentor, but also by the whole school. What we especially noticed when listening to Yael was her respectful attitude to her students, and her confidence to talk about how and why she taught the way she taught her students. We see this as an indication of confidence in herself as teacher and true dedication to her job. We were happy to learn she sees her future in education.

References

Castro, A. J., Kelly, J., & Shih, M. (2010). Resilience strategies for new teachers in high-needs areas. *Teaching and Teacher Education, 26*(3), 622–629.

Darom, D. (2000). Humanistic values education. In M. Leicester & S. Modgil (Eds.), *Politics, education and citizenship* (pp. 16–26). London: Routledge.

Freire, P. (1973). *Education for critical consciousness* (Vol. 1). London: Bloomsbury Publishing.

Gu, Q., & Day, C. (2007). Teachers resilience: A necessary condition for effectiveness. *Teaching and Teacher Education, 23*, 1302–1316.

Hargreaves, A. (2000). Mixed emotions: Teachers' perceptions of their interactions with students. *Teaching and Teacher Education, 16*(8), 811–826.

Hargreaves, A., & Tucker, E. (1991). Teaching and guilt: Exploring the feelings of teaching. *Teaching and Teacher Education, 7*(5–6), 491–505.

Roness, D., & Smith, K. (2009). Postgraduate certificate in Education (PGCE) and student motivation. *European Journal of Teacher Education, 32*(2), 111–135.

Smith, K., Ulvik, M., & Helleve, I. (2013). *Førstereisen—Lærdom hentet fra nye læreres fortellinger* [The First Journey—Lessons learned from newly qualified teachers]. Oslo: Gyldendal Akademisk.

Ulvik, M., Smith, K., & Helleve, I. (2009). Novice in secondary school. The coin has two sides. *Teaching and Teacher Education, 25*(6), 835–842.

Watt, H. M., Richardson, P. W., Klusmann, U., Kunter, M., Beyer, B., Trautwein, U., & Baumert, J. (2012). Motivations for choosing teaching as a career: An international comparison using the FIT-Choice scale. *Teaching and Teacher Education, 28*(6), 791–805.

PART 5

The Norwegian Teacher Education Context

Introduction to Part 5: The Norwegian Context

Marit Ulvik

Traditionally there have been two different routes to become a teacher in Norway. University colleges have offered a four-year teacher education programme for primary and lower secondary school. The universities have offered a one-year postgraduate teacher education programme for secondary schools and from 2004 also a five-year integrated teacher education programme that leads to a master's degree in a school subject. The situation today is a bit more complex due to the fact that some university colleges have become universities and a National Curriculum has been implemented with more overlap between different programmes. Furthermore, from 2019 all teacher education in Norway requires a master's degree.

The Norwegian teachers in our sample are educated from a university and work in upper secondary school (years 11–13, often referred to as year one, two and three) with students between 16 and 19 years old. Compulsory primary and lower secondary schooling in Norway lasts ten years, and with less than 3% of students in private schools, most students go to their local schools for the 10 first years. Furthermore, all pupils have a right to three years in upper secondary education. Academic and vocational programmes are usually offered in the same schools and can all lead into higher education which implies that academic subjects are offered in both programmes. Students in the academic programme finish school after three years, vocational students go to school for two years, then they work as apprentices for two more years before getting a certificate of completed apprenticeship. Alternatively, they can add an extra year in school instead of being an apprentice and thereby get access to higher education. Almost every student from lower secondary enrolls in upper secondary education or training (about 98% in 2012), which means that teachers in upper secondary school encounter a broad cohort of students. One of the main objectives of primary and secondary education in Norway is that all pupils who are able to do so should complete upper secondary education and obtain qualifications that will prepare them for further study or work. It should be mentioned, however, that drop out has been a problem in upper secondary schools and critics have been raised against theorising vocational training.

The educational system in Norway aims to foster humanistic values and at the same time there has been an increased emphasis on measurability. The last years there has been a raised focus on international comparisons and tests, and a National Curriculum (The Knowledge Promotion Reform) from 2006 emphasising the integration of basic skills into all subjects in all levels with focus on achievement and results. The basic skills are: the ability to express oneself orally, the ability to read, numeracy, the ability to express oneself in writing, and the ability to use digital tools. One might say that there exists a tension between Norway's traditional humanistic and social democratic values and the new emphasis on measurable outcomes. Some of the government's suggestions to deal with the relative lack of academic achievement in the schools revealed in international tests like PISA, is to improve the quality of teacher education, to increase the recruitment to the teaching profession, to offer mentoring to newly qualified teachers and to establish the development of a national graduate school in teacher education (NAFOL).

To improve the quality of teacher education, new teacher education programmes have been implemented (2010, level 1–10 and 2014, level 8–13). The emphases in the new programmes are on subject knowledge, teaching skills and the quality of studies, but unlike for example England there are greater emphasis on research. Current policy will furthermore bring about a gradual implementation to a five-year master's degree for all teacher educations, an arrangement that requires teacher educators with a doctorate. The question is if student teachers are willing to study five years to become teachers. The status and popularity of the teaching profession in Norway has dropped over time, and it is today possible to get into teacher education with mediocre grades from upper secondary school. The government has established a partnership (GNIST), an initiative among others to raise the status of the teaching profession and to improve the recruitment to teacher education. There is today a shortfall of teachers, and by 2020 it is calculated that Norway will lack 11.000 qualified teachers. The unemployment rate in Norway is less than 4%, and it is easy for people with higher education to get a well-paid job in the private sector.

Especially student teachers from the universities with a master's degree have a lot of job opportunities, and to start as newly qualified teachers is considered quite challenging. Even if there is a shortfall of teachers, it is difficult to get a permanent teaching position in the cities, and a lot of teachers in secondary schools have to start as substitute teachers and to teach subjects they are not qualified for (more than 20%). In addition they have to work hard to prove their suitability for permanent employment. In Norway, new teachers have until now not had any formal induction or reduction in teaching during the first year, but are expected to shoulder the same responsibilities as their experienced colleagues from the first day. Despite a government decision to offer mentoring to all new teachers from 2010, support has so far been rather discretionary, depending on the school's leadership and goodwill of colleagues.

CHAPTER 10

Endre's Story: You Have to Try out Different Things

Endre works in an upper secondary school in Norway (years 11–13 – called years one, two and three) with students between 16 and 19 years old. In Norway, most upper secondary schools offer both vocational and academic programmes, and Endre teaches English in both programmes. Students in the academic programme finish school after three years. Vocational students go to school for two years and then work as apprentices for two more years before getting a certificate of completed apprenticeship. Alternatively, they can supplement their vocational school training with an extra year in school instead of being an apprentice, and they thereby become eligible for higher education. Teachers in academic subjects are educated in two subjects, and as student teachers, they have their practicum in these subjects. Like Endre, however, some teachers choose to add an extra year and an extra subject to their portfolio to make it easier to get a job. Endre explains how he experienced his start as a teacher.

I am educated as a "lektor" (a Norwegian designation for teachers with a master's degree) and I have a master's degree in history. I am also educated in religion and in English. All in all, I have a seven year-long education from the university.

There are lot of teachers in my family, on both sides, so I suppose that is the reason why I became a teacher myself. I have always heard: *Oh, I'm sure you will become a teacher*, and at first, I thought that it never would happen. But after some years at the university I wondered whether I might want to become a part of academia. *No*, I did not want the continual pressure of having to perform academically. Later, however, I decided to first finish a master's degree and thereafter a PGCE (postgraduate teacher education) and become a teacher. Nevertheless, until the PGCE, I was still in doubt about my decision, because I did not know if I could manage the teaching role in practice.

1 My Classes

For the time being, I only teach English, my minor subject. I have slowly but surely increased my job from 25% to 80% of a full position. The 25% was all I got initially. I applied for many teaching vacancies, including in lower secondary school. I took this job because I knew it was in a very big school and that I would likely be offered more classes in the course of the first year. After only a couple of days, I had a 40% post; and after Christmas 80%. I do not know, however, if I will have a job for the next school year.

Now (in May), I have different kinds of classes: two vocational first-year classes with very nice students, then I have two classes in technology and industrial production. In English, they are merged into one class with 28 boys, and that is quite challenging, among other things because the school introduced textbooks in vocational English this year. Before that, they had digital resources. It took me some time to discover the change, and because of that, I got off to a somewhat messy start.

It was very difficult for me as a new teacher to familiarise myself with everything, like the curriculum and how things were organised in the school. During my PGCE, I did not have English didactics; I had didactics and practicum in my two other subjects. So my minor subject, which I was not certified to teach, is the only one I am teaching at the moment. It took me several weeks just to get started.

Then I have a second-year class that I took over from another teacher after Christmas. I am the third teacher they have had. That is a challenging class with some challenging students, maybe because I have them the two last lessons on Fridays.

The last class I got was a year two class in the academic programme; I teach them International English. The group has five lessons a week. I like to have the class, but find it challenging because my background in English is limited and it is not easy to take over a subject in the middle of the year, especially now just before exams when we are supposed to revise. It is difficult to revise things I have not taught myself. Altogether, I have six different classes. What is good about vocational classes is that they actually come to the lessons. They do not want any black marks against them, because then it would be difficult for them to be accepted for an apprenticeship. It is more important for them to avoid absences than to achieve good grades in English. In the academic class, I do not think I have had a single lesson when all the students were present.

In the first-year classes, I have a very good relationship with the students. I enjoy teaching them the first year because they do not have an exam in English this year, and they do not have all-day tests. My only obligation is to get through about half the curriculum. I have three lessons a week and the classes are always small. In the second year, two classes are merged in my school, and the students have their exam in English this year, so the second year is more stressful.

2 Ups and Downs

Looking back, I think my first year has been okay. You try out different ways of teaching. You cannot predict the outcome, but you try different strategies. I have learned not to be afraid of failing. If I fail totally in one lesson, then I try to do better the next time. I have never taught several bad lessons consecutively. I have always managed to adjust. That is what you have to do all the time – try out different ways of teaching and of assessing. When I did my practicum, I carefully prepared all the lessons and wanted to show the students how much I knew. Now I know that it is equally effective to let the students do a large part of the work. That insight relieved me of a burden.

What I enjoy is the contact with students, especially one to one. I become acquainted with them, and it gives me empowering experiences to have a good dialogue with students. I think I am quite good at establishing relationships with them. I learn their names rather quickly. I put time and effort into it and I use the names a lot in the first lessons. I am better at learning the names of my students than my colleagues. Luckily, I am not a form master because the school tries not to put that responsibility on new teachers. But I have had dialogues related to the subject matter with all my students (which all teachers at the upper secondary level have to do), and when they have oral presentations, I like to give them oral feedback one to one, and I really enjoy that. In the International English class, the students had two presentations, and I noticed that many of them improved a lot from the first to the second time because they had listened to the feedback I gave them. It was very satisfying to see how they had picked up from the feedback and improved. It gave me a very good feeling.

Marking papers is what I like least, spending long evenings at home doing marking. Last week, two of the classes had all-day tests, and I got 50 tests to mark. That will take some time and it can become quite boring.

In vocational English, the cooperation between colleagues shows room for improvement. Some of my colleagues want to work alone. Regardless of where I work next year, I will do something about it and make my own group. This year I missed having people to ask about details. It was only by coincidence, for example, that I learned about the textbooks. There should have been better cooperation between the teachers. I do not know why it is lacking, but one reason may be that many new teachers are given the vocational classes and there is no one really in charge. I for one enjoy the vocational classes provided they are not the only classes I have.

One thing that has made an impression on me is meeting students who behave poorly and do not seem to want to achieve anything, and then participating in class meetings with all the teachers of the class and learning about the students' backgrounds. Some of these students have been let down during their whole life, in every way. You feel so sorry for them. If some of those students do not appear to want to get anything out of my lessons, I try to talk to them in private. I tell them that I know it is hard, but that we should try together to make it work. There are limits, however, to how far I can go, but I make an extra effort for students who have a hard time.

When it comes to classroom management, I have a natural bonus, as a tall man, because my height gives me automatic authority. Few students are taller than I am. I also think I manage the classroom well because I have a good relationship with the students. I like to talk to them myself if there is a problem, but sometimes I will go to their form master. Especially in the merged second-year class, I enjoy good cooperation with the two class teachers. They are very good at working with the subject teachers. Another thing I can do when students do not behave, is to write them up. First, I give them a warning, and most students will then adjust their behaviour.

I asked one student, maybe the most problematic one I have had, why he was not doing anything in English lessons. Then he told me that he had never had English before. He had gone through primary and lower secondary school without English. During his first year at upper secondary, he was not given a grade in English, but this second year he would have to sit for the exam. I was so surprised, and suddenly this became my responsibility. I spoke with the guidance counsellor, and now it has been decided that he cannot have a grade in English because he has not done anything, only disrupted the lessons.

A good experience I had recently was to try out a new way of assessing which involved a one-to-one conversation in English about a book the students had read. It was hard to do it because it took time, but it was so enjoyable to listen to the students and try to have a real conversation with them. It was great to do something different. Because I do not have anything from my practicum to draw on in English, I have to reinvent the wheel all the time. But since I have different classes on the same level, I can use the same planning in different classes, although with some adjustments.

3 Support

When it comes to support, I think it is my responsibility to ask for it. I have tried to improve cooperation with the other English teacher in the vocational classes, and we have now prepared a joint all-day test in English. I also communicate well with the other new teachers, the ones who are my age. We sometimes exchange ideas about things and find out things together. Furthermore, one teacher acts as a mentor, although not from the start. I can understand why there is attrition in the teaching profession. Being thrown into it is hard. A mentor arrangement would have been very good – to have someone you can talk to and ask questions. Initially it was not easy for me. There are different buildings in the school, and I did not work every day. But I have a good relationship with the department head, and I have asked her lots of questions, and she has helped me a lot.

The start could have been better organised, especially the first days, which are planning days for the teachers. On one of those days, I could not do anything because I did not have a computer, textbooks or my own workplace. I wish that things were better organised before I started, and that I initially had more basic information. I would also have appreciated knowing whom I could ask. However, I cooperate well with one of the English teachers. She has had the subject before, and she has been very helpful for me as a new teacher. Most colleagues are very helpful when you consult them.

4   From Student to Teacher

Being a teacher has given me a circadian rhythm for the first time in my life. I really had problems with that as a student. Why get up in the morning when you do not have to? Now you have to, and that is okay. Then you are tired in the evenings. You have a rhythm during the day, during the week, very good, actually. You get a salary. Things are easier when you have routines to follow. You do not have to worry about an exam, either. I have even worn my best clothes, even though I did not have to. I joke with my colleagues that it reminds me of being a grown-up.

I think that the PGCE could have prepared me better. Practicum was very useful. Subject didactics were important. Pedagogy (educational theory/general didactics) was more difficult to put into practice. There was a lot of theory and I felt that some of lecturers really did not have enough experience from the actual school environment. Nevertheless, I was lucky enough to have a seminar leader who had been a schoolteacher for many years and had many examples to draw on. During the past year, I became tired of being a student, which I never thought would happen. I did a count and found that I had been in education for the past 20 years. So I was not very motivated.

5   The Future

Next year I will change my planning technique and make more long-term plans, not in detail, but rough plans. Then I will not have to decide for every lesson. I would like to continue to have good relationships with students, and I want to improve when it comes to cooperation with other teachers and make my own groups. The group does not have to be very formal and does not have to meet at a specified time every week, but for example every second week. Maybe we could have some common frames when we decide grades, and we could give each other tips. It would make things easier.

I think I will continue to be a teacher, but it depends on what happens with my role as a teacher. I know that some changes might be implemented that affect working hours. But I do not think I would then automatically leave teaching, because I do not know what else I would do. I enjoy being a teacher, and look forward to going to work every day. Sometimes it is a bit scary and you wonder whether what you have planned will be okay. Often it is okay, even though it may not be perfect every time. I learned that from my practicum. I used to be so nervous before every lesson back then. When I look back on it now, I think that I had no reason to be so afraid. The lessons were not very good, but I can see that I learned a lot.

To get a full-time, permanent job as a teacher is not easy, and at the moment, it is quite stressful. I have a lot of marking to do, and at the same time I have to apply for a new job for next school year. Not knowing what to do in August is worrisome.

6 What Does Endre's Story Tell?

6.1 *A Messy Start*

The transition from being taught to teaching others is described in the literature as an identity shift and a vulnerable phase in teachers' lives (Bullough, 2005; Langdon, 2007). Will the students recognise the new teacher? Will he be included among the staff? The phase has different labels like cultural shock, practice shock and transfer shock (Caspersen & Raaen, 2014). The labels express that the transition from education to work is experienced as challenging. Transition is a challenge in other professions as well, but teachers seem to have lower levels of follow-up than other professions (ibid). Furthermore, even if people have observed teaching for years, they seem to be surprised by how it actually is to teach (Smith, Ulvik, & Helleve, 2013).

We learn from Endre's story that starting to work as a teacher even has an impact on his way of living as well as how he dresses. Now he definitely can be perceived as a responsible grown-up with fixed routines—and he likes it that way. He is ready for work after many years within the educational system. Unfortunately, he is not able to get a permanent or a full time position and typically has to accept work as a substitute teacher. Despite the teacher shortage in Norway, it can be difficult to get a job in the cities, especially in upper secondary school. However, it is debatable that Endre's start can be described as a shock. On the one hand, Endre has to find out things by himself. It is hard for him to familiarise himself with everything, and he has the feeling that he has to reinvent the wheel. On the other hand, he manages quite well. In the literature, practice shock relates to the discrepancy between an ideal perception of teaching and the reality teachers may experience in an early career phase (Kyriacou & Kunc, 2007; Smethem, 2007; Johnsen et al., 2014). In Endre's case, he thinks his first year has been okay and he seems to be able to cope, even from the start. However, we should bear in mind that in the beginning of his first year of teaching, Endre did not have a full-time job. He started out with a 25-percent position. Furthermore, the interview took place towards the end of his first year. He might have perceived his job differently during the first period than he did in retrospect. Teachers' professional development is described in the literature as following a learning curve in which they first focus on themselves and on being accepted, and then on the teaching and finally on the students (e.g. Fuller & Brown, 1975; Flores & Day, 2006). Endre tells that it relieved him from a burden to change from wanting to show the students how clever he was to understanding that it is the students who should be allowed to do much of the work themselves. This change happened for Endre already in his practicum. However, he most likely had a harder time initially than at the end of his first year.

Although Endre enjoys being a teacher and seems to manage, the start of his professional career is far from optimal; this is unfortunately quite common for new teachers. Endre had to start as a substitute teacher and to teach classes many experienced teachers do not want to teach. For example, Endre, like other new teachers, had to teach vocational classes that are often expected to be on a lower level than academic classes. He also taught his minor subject in which his knowledge was limited. Furthermore, taking over classes in the middle of the year can be an extra challenge. The students have already got used to another teacher's style and the new teacher has to familiarise himself with what the students have already been through. Endre felt as if he was thrown into teaching, and when he eventually got a mentor, he had already managed the first period by himself. However, he strongly recommends having an appointed mentor to ask all the "silly" questions. All newly qualified teachers in Norway are supposed to be offered mentoring the first year. There are, however, no requirements in terms of content or volume of mentoring. Substitute or part-time teachers in particular tend to fall between two stools, so that even if they get a mentor, the scope of the mentoring may vary. Furthermore, novices often want help with solving practical and technical problems (Caspersen & Raaen, 2014). In turn, they are often afraid of disturbing their colleagues with all their practical questions, and appreciate someone who is paid to help them (Smith, Ulvik, & Helleve, 2013).

From research, we know that leaving new teachers on their own is not a good idea, neither for them nor for their students. The attrition rate in teaching is high (Wang, Odell, & Schwille, 2008; Roness, 2011). Many teachers leave the profession during the first three to five years, a decision often triggered by their first teaching experiences (Achinstein, 2006; Rots et al., 2007). Moreover, practice shock often results in traditional pedagogical behaviour on the part of new teachers (Rots et al., 2013). Building on their own experiences, teachers tend to teach as they have been taught. Furthermore, new teachers have a tendency to be rigid and to carry out rule-governed practices related to their uncertainty (Caspersen & Raaen, 2014). Teachers who are insecure are less likely to take risks, but might discipline students contrary their own ideals, and they tend to choose teacher-centred methods (Brouwer & Korthagen, 2005). Conversely, new teachers who experience that they are mastering the profession become more open minded and connected to teaching (Hoy & Spero, 2005). The first stage in teaching is also described as an important learning stage in which teachers have to find their own way (Caspersen & Raaen, 2014; Fresko & Alhija, 2009). Often they are socialised into the existing school culture because of workload and time pressure rather than being offered time to think things through and find their own answers. In the initial phase, a good relationship with students and a supportive atmosphere at school play a crucial role (Flores & Day, 2006). Endre did not experience a supportive atmosphere among his experienced colleagues. However, what is detrimental to new teachers is not the occurrence of negative events, but the absence of positive experiences (Morgan, Ludlow, Kitching, O'Leary, & Clarke, 2010). What meant a lot for Endre and helped him through his ordeal was the positive relationship he had with his students.

6.2   *Relationships*

Endre describes himself as good at making relationships. He describes that he was nervous during practicum, but he obviously has had some positive experiences that gave him confidence. He enjoys talking to students and makes an effort to learn their names. He does not leave this to chance. He is also conscious about how he relates to students. He describes that he feels sorry for them when he learns more about their background and he tries to treat them in an understanding way – within limits. The literature describes it as crucial the first year to establish a close relationship with the students and to succeed in that respect (Flores, 2006; Hirschkorn, 2009). Teachers' motivation is most often related to having an impact on students, and it is not surprising that we found in a previous study among new teachers that critical incidents often were related to relationships with students (Ulvik, Smith, & Helleve, 2017).

From a student's point of view, recognition is important, as well as having a feeling of being seen and understood by the teacher. Roach and Lewis (2011) found that students characterise their teachers by two distinct styles of discipline. One style is 'coercive' in nature and is dependent on punishment and aggressive teacher behaviour. The other style is 'relationship'-based and dependent on the use of discussion, hinting, recognition and requires involvement. Teachers' disciplinary styles seem to affect students and their ability to develop responsible behaviour. Students who are the objects of the latter disciplinary style generally act more responsibly than do students with authoritarian teachers. Recognising and rewarding positive behaviour of both individual students and the class as a whole results in positive benefits in terms of building relationships and establishing an environment of trust and respect. Recognition creates an opportunity for the teachers to balance sanctions with positive reinforcement. Endre seems to succeed in establishing a relation-based style. Hearing the teacher addressing them by name, talking to them and trying to see everyone individually, the students feel included. Moreover, Endre finds it easier to establish a good relationship with students he gets to know from the very start of the school year. He also says that it helps that his vocational students do not have an exam in English, the subject he teaches, during their first year in upper secondary school. The pressure on achieving is thereby reduced. Consequently, schools can influence the relationship between teacher and students by how they organise classes and teachers. Successful student experiences build teachers' confidence and self-efficacy, which is crucial during the first years in the profession (Roach & Lewis, 2011). Confident teachers more likely take risks and try to improve their teaching. Positive experiences with students may be one important factor explaining why Endre enjoys teaching. The practice shock is described as an inability to act and lack of opportunity to control the situation (Caspersen & Raaen, 2014). Endre has some kind of control and he manages to act. He seems like a resilient teacher.

6.3   *Resilience*
Resilience is not about escaping negative feelings, but about recovering quickly (Gu & Day, 2007). It involves developing personal courage and the capacity to move into challenging situations (Le Cornu, 2009). One characteristic of Endre is that he is not afraid of failing, and failure does not stop him for trying again. Resilience is described as a protective factor in novice teachers' development

(Beltman, Mansfield, & Price, 2011). Johnsen et al. (2014) describe resilience as an interaction between internal resources and external environment. It is enhanced by strength of beliefs and aspiration. Even if Endre fails totally, he tries to do better next time and one can ask why he does not give up. What strengthens his courage might be that he also experiences improvement. Resilience is the outcome of a dynamic relationship between individual risk and protective factors (Beltman, Mansfield, & Price, 2011). In Endre's case he manages what is important for teachers, the immediate classroom context – for example, managing challenging behaviour, meeting diverse student needs, forming positive relationships with students and staff (ibid). He takes initiatives. When his colleagues will not cooperate, he finds his own partnerships among other new teachers. He really tries to make the best of things and says that it is his own responsibility to ask questions. At the same time, he also thinks that the school has not been sufficiently supportive. Nevertheless, instead of leaving it to the school, he asks what he can do about it. Although some colleagues did not want to cooperate, he finds it necessary to mention that he had a supportive leader. Resilience is enhanced when leaders take a personal interest in new teachers' welfare and development (Peters & Pearce, 2012; Pogodzinski, Youngs, Frank, & Belman, 2012).

Endre, like all teachers, has his ups and downs, but the positive experiences seem to prevail over the negative ones. However, the fact that Endre's experiences end on the positive side is not thanks to the school. It is more thanks to himself and chance occurrences. The school eventually provided him with a mentor and he fortunately had a supportive leader; otherwise, he was left to fend for himself. He tried to make the best of the situation and was willing to try out different ways of teaching.

We learn from Endre's story that the school should have given him a mentor from the start, even though he only had a small, part-time position. Both Endre and his students might have benefited from having had a mentor. He would have been spared from reinventing the wheel all the time and spending valuable time only to find out what a mentor could easily have told him in the first place. Furthermore, there could have been more cooperation among teachers. It would have been easier for Endre to plan teaching in a subject in which he has limited knowledge together with more skilled teachers. They might even learn from him, for example from his engagement and willingness to improve and try out new things.

What really bothers Endre at the end of his first year is that he does not know if he has a job for the next year. He shares his situation with other teachers in this book. Trying to get a permanent position, teachers in many different countries accept poor working conditions and try to make the best of the situation. When there is always a new teacher ready and eager to find a job, schools lack the incentive to improve. In the end, it is students who have to pay for the high turnover rate (Ronfeldt, Loeb & Wyckoff, 2013).

7 Conclusion

Endre manages his first year without a permanent position and is still motivated. He has had his ups and downs, but thanks to his own initiatives and ability to establish relationships with students, positive experiences seem to have a dominating influence. What he misses, is more cooperation among teachers and an appointed mentor. Furthermore, if he has to apply for a job a third time, he might be one of those who manages and enjoys teaching, but still leaves the profession. Listening to Endre's story, it is striking how the school seems to prioritize their permanent staff and leaves the tasks that are left to the newcomers. From Endre we learn that cooperation, mentoring and a reasonable job could make it easier to work as a newly qualified teacher. These are expectations that should be possible for schools to live up to.

References

Achinstein, B. (2006). New teacher and mentor political literacy: Reading, navigating and transforming induction contexts. *Teachers and Teaching: Theory and Practice, 12*(2), 123–138.

Beltman, S., Mansfield, C., & Price, A. (2011). Thriving not just surviving: A review of research on teacher resilience. *Educational Research Review, 6*(3), 185–207.

Brouwer, N., & Korthagen, F. (2005). Can teacher education make a difference? *American Educational Research Journal, 42*(1), 153–224.

Bullough, R. V. (2005). Being and becoming a mentor: School-based teacher educators and teacher educator identity. *Teaching and Teacher Education, 21*, 143–155.

Caspersen, J., & Raaen, F. D. (2014). Novice teachers and how they cope. *Teachers and Teaching: Theory and Practice, 20*(2), 189–211.

Flores, M. A. (2006). Being a novice teacher in two different settings: Struggles, continuities, and discontinuities. *Teachers College Record, 108*(10), 2021–2052.

Flores, M. A., & Day, C. (2006). Contexts which shape and reshape new teachers' identities: A multi-perspective study. *Teaching and Teacher Education, 22*, 219–232.

Fresko, B., & Alhija, F. N. A. (2009). When intentions and reality clash: Inherent implementation difficulties of an induction program for new teachers. *Teaching and Teacher Education, 25*(2), 278–284.

Fuller, F. F., & Brown, O. H. (1975). Becoming a teacher. In K. Ryan (Ed.), *Teacher education, the 74th yearbook of the National Society for the study of education*. Chicago, IL: University of Chicago Press.

Gu, Q., & Day, C. (2007). Teachers' resilience: A necessary condition for effectiveness. *Teaching and Teacher Education, 23*(8), 1302–1316.

Hirschkorn, M. (2009). Student teacher relationship and teacher induction: Ben's story. *Teacher Development, 13*(3), 205–217.

Hoy, A. W., & Spero, R. B. (2005). Changes in teacher efficacy during the early years of teaching: A comparison on four measures. *Teacher and Teacher Education, 21*, 343–356.

Johnsen, B., Down, B., Le Cornu, R., Peters, J., Sullivan, A., Pearce, J., & Hunter, J. (2014). Promoting early career teacher resilience: A framework for understanding and acting. *Teachers and Teaching, 20*(5), 530–546.

Kyriacou, C., & Kunc, R. (2007). Beginning teachers' expectations of teaching. *Teaching and Teacher Education, 23*, 1246–1257.

Langdon, F. J. (2007). *Beginning teacher learning and professional development: An analysis of induction programmes* (PhD thesis). The University of Waikato, Hamilton, New Zealand.

Le Cornu, R. (2009). Building resilience in pre-service teachers. *Teaching and Teacher Education, 25*(5), 717–723.

Morgan, M., Ludlow, L., Kitching, K., O'Leary, M., & Clarke, A. (2010). What makes teachers tick? Sustaining events in new teachers' lives. *British Educational Research Journal, 36*(2), 191–208.

Peters, J., & Pearce, J. (2012). Relationships and early career teacher resilience: A role for school principals. *Teachers and Teaching: Theory and Practice, 18*(2), 249–262.

Pogodzinski, B., Youngs, P., Frank, K. A., & Belman, D. (2012). Administrative climate and novices' intent to remain teaching. *The Elementary School Journal, 113*(2), 252–275.

Roach, J., & Lewis, R. (2011) Teachers' views on the impact of classroom management on student responsibility. *Australian Journal of Education, 55*(2), 132–146.

Roness, D. (2011). Still motivated? The motivation for teaching during the second year in the profession. *Teaching and Teacher Education, 27*, 628–638.

Ronfeldt, M., Loeb, S., & Wyckoff, J. (2013). How teacher turnover harms student achievement. *American Educational Research Journal, 50*(1), 4–36.

Rots, I., Aelterman, A., Vlerick, P., & Vermeulen, K. (2007). Teacher education, graduates' teaching commitment and entrance into the teaching profession. *Teaching and Teacher Education, 23*(5), 543–556.

Smethem, L. (2007). Retention and intention in teaching careers: Will the new generation stay? *Teachers and Teaching: Theory and Practice, 13*(5), 465–480.

Smith, K., Ulvik, M., & Helleve, I. (2013). *Førstereisen – Lærdom hentet fra nye læreres fortellinger* [First Journey – Lessons learned from novice teachers]. Oslo: Gyldendal.

Ulvik, M., Smith, K., & Helleve, I. (2017). Ethical aspects of professional dilemmas in the first year of teaching. *Professional Development in Education, 43*(2), 236–252.

Wang, J., Odell, S. J., & Schwille, S. A. (2008). Effects of teacher induction on beginning teachers' teaching: A critical review of the literature. *Journal of Teacher Education, 59*(2), 132–152.

CHAPTER 11

Eva's Story: Critical Thinking, a challenge and an Opportunity

1   Becoming a Teacher

This is the seventh school I have worked in. I have some experience from before I took my PGCE (postgraduate teacher education), both from primary and different secondary schools. Last year, after the PGCE, I worked 40% in an upper secondary school and worked in addition as a substitute teacher in different schools. This year I have a 74% position in an upper secondary school, and I teach three classes in Norwegian in the academic programme, two first-year classes and one second-year class. I could choose between two posts, and I chose the one that was not permanent, because I wanted to be in upper secondary school and because the job description was very clear. With Norwegian as one of my subjects, I do not think I will have a problem getting a job next year, and hopefully the job I have will become permanent.

I became a teacher because I had not found anything better to do, and I like it. My parents are also teachers. I thought about being a journalist or something, but not seriously. I have enjoyed the first half year in the job I currently have. Some teachers complain that the job takes over their lives, but I am very busy at home, so my work has not taken over my entire life. I have a child, and we recently bought an apartment after a lot of viewing and stress. So going to school and meeting the students has been purely positive.

2   Collaboration or Sharing

However, there has been some frustration at work as well. There are many men in upper secondary school who know (or think they know) how to teach, and the young teachers look up to the more experienced ones. Therefore, there is not much cooperation, as I see it. There is a lot of sharing, but very little accepting. There is a lot of goodwill, but everyone tends to want to have things the way they are used to. Since I have worked in other schools and have written an essay about cooperation, I know that cooperation can vary from school to school. In other schools, I have seen people working together on assessment and making plans and tests together. In my last job, I made a very useful and efficient plan for half a year with two of my colleagues. I had to jump into something that was new to me and it was challenging, but I learned a lot and I liked it very much. Three of us followed the same plan, and I felt secure because I was not alone in the planning. In this school, everyone develops their own plans. I have a leader of my department, though, who has said that I can ask him about anything. He is very nice and forthcoming, but also very busy. So I prefer to ask my colleagues.

3 Likes and Dislikes

What I like best about my job is when the students think independently and come up with their own contributions, and when we create situations together that are not only controlled by me, the teacher, but also by the students, who are allowed to come up with their own reflections. I also very much like to listen to students and learn how they would like to have things done.

What I do not like is the long working days. However, in upper secondary it feels less busy than in primary and lower secondary school. There is a lot to do here as well, but it is not so intense. Still, you sometimes feel powerless. I cope, however, because I do not have a full-time position.

I feel secure in this school, and the students do well. But last year I had some classes in the vocational programme, some of the toughest groups. Then I felt as though I was in a foreign world. So to have chosen this job with fewer problems seems kind of cowardly. But I enjoy being here.

4 Critical Incidents

Last year I had some experiences that really affected me. For example, I had a class with several students with different diagnoses, among others ADHD (Attention Deficit Hyperactivity Disorder). It was quite crazy to experience that group. I have no bad memories, however. Individual students were okay. But some episodes were quite tough. One of the students was manipulative and knew what buttons to press to disturb students and teachers. It was very special to discover how I became fond of the student and at the same time saw the consequences of his behaviour in other people. One problem, as I saw it, was how the school treated the challenges made by the student and the class. I felt that they took the wrong approach. They were too hard on the boy and treated him the wrong way, even though they did get help and advice from the educational and psychological counselling. It made an impression on me to feel that what they were doing was wrong. They tried to isolate the student, which did not work at all. I got along well with him because he also had a lot of charm. These boys were just a group of pubertal youths.

Another episode that made a big impression happened in a Norwegian class where I was reading a short story. Suddenly one of the boys interrupted me and said that I could not read the story in that class because it was about a black person and we had a black person in the class. The boy had a tendency to be challenging, but he was also honest, so I did not know if he perceived the short story as racist or if he was simply challenging me. The story was not racist, of course, but I had been in doubt about whether I should read it or not, and had asked some of my colleagues for advice. And what if the students thought the story was racist, even if it was not? There and then, I became very insecure and did not know what to do. I ended up asking the class, and told them that I would not read the story aloud if anyone felt offended. Then some of the students wanted me to continue, which I chose to do. The students then learned how the story ended and probably understood that it was not racist. I think that was one of my toughest experiences. I felt completely shaky and vulnerable, but also experienced that things often turn out all right and that it is possible to ask students, and to be in dialogue with them. So now I remember the situation as tough, but positive.

What I have learned so far is that as a teacher you develop as a person. Now I have become a real grown-up. What I would like to improve, is in doing more for vulnerable students.

5   What Does Eva's Story Tell?

Like many other newly qualified teachers, Eva has parents who are teachers and she obviously has a positive impression of the profession. When she had to decide what occupation she wanted to pursue, she considered other alternatives, but she was not able to think of anything she wanted more than teaching. She really enjoys it, and like other teachers in our sample, she especially likes to be with her students.

As a new teacher, Eva wants to have a manageable job and she takes steps to get that kind of job, even if it means refusing a permanent position. Just after graduation, Eva worked for a short period as a substitute teacher. When she applied for her first one-year appointment, she was aware, based on her experiences, of the kind of job she wanted to accept. It is thanks to Eva's own decisions that her entry into teaching became mainly a positive experience.

5.1 Collaboration or Sharing

Eva is satisfied with her students, but is a little annoyed by some of her male colleagues and their attitude when it comes to collaboration. From previous experience, she knows that some teachers collaborate quite well and plan their teaching together. We know from research that there are different attitudes towards collaboration and further professional learning among teachers. Hargreaves found in 1994 that there is a more individualistic school culture in upper secondary school, a finding in line with Eva's experience a couple of decades later. A group of researchers identified in their study three different views on learning among teachers (Van Eekelen, Vermunt, & Boshuizen, 2006):
– Those who are eager to learn.
– Those who see challenges, but wonder how they should learn.
– Those who do not see any need for learning.

The first group is open minded and interested in learning new things. The next group wants to learn, but expects others to take the initiative. Eva's colleagues seem to be in the latter group. They have found their way of teaching and it works for them. They do not see any need to change. Whether this is more common among male teachers, as Eva suggests, we do not know. Dewy claimed in 1933 that it requires hard work to change old beliefs. Even though they do not want to change, Eva's colleagues are friendly and willing to share. But by knowing best how to teach, they do not recognize Eva as contributor. It is decisive in the professional development of new teachers that they be acknowledged by their colleagues (Engvik, 2014). In her previous job, she felt she was part of a team. It is interesting that Eva differentiates between collaboration and sharing. Collaboration is mutual; sharing can be a unilateral gesture. New teachers want to be accepted and not be seen merely as helpless. Emphasis on helping newcomers may undermine their role as contributors (Ulvik & Langørgen, 2012). Furthermore, school development may suffer from not getting access to alternative practices and different perspectives.

Teachers are more likely to develop in collaborating cultures (Flores & Day, 2006). It is easier to acquire teacher identity and to manage the job (Caspersen & Raaen, 2014; Rippon & Martin, 2006). Collaboration presupposes dialogue. In addition, dialogues require participants to mediate between more than one perspective: self-perspective and other-perspective (Penlington, 2008). When challenged by others, one can move beyond one's own level. New teachers do lack experience, but they bring in a view from the outside that can be useful. Furthermore, teachers can be good at different things in different ways (Eisner, 2002). Especially in a changing society, young people may have something to teach the older generation. A previous study found that the new teachers themselves think they are better than experienced colleagues are when it comes to ICT and communication with young people because of more common frames of reference (Ulvik & Langørgen, 2012). Learning from each other is a contrast to the notion that there is one 'best' way of teaching, and mutual learning benefits everyone.

Collaboration can, however, be both a complicating factor and an important tool for learning (Dobber, Akkerman, Verloop, & Vermunt, 2012). It can sometimes be stressful (Caspersen & Raaen, 2014; Smith, Ulvik, & Helleve, 2013). New teachers want to manage, and being in groups with experienced teachers can be intimidating; the newcomers might feel that they are not good enough. Collaboration presupposes trust and a good relationship, something that might develop over time among people who interact and recognise each other.

5.2   *Critical Incidents That Make the Teacher Reflect*

The informants in this book were asked to tell about critical incidents. These are situations that have a decisive meaning for the teacher involved, although the episodes may be perceived as marginal by those who are not involved (Tripp, 1994). The meaning of an incident is often understood only in retrospect. Critical incidents depend on how we look at and interpret a situation; it is a matter of value judgements (Nilsson, 2009). However, it is often not easy to identify single situations because critical incidents might be varied and ongoing. Researchers therefore recommend instead to look for affective episodes that happen every day (Mansfield, Beltman, & Price, 2014). Nevertheless, Eva was an informant who was able to identify single episodes.

Eva got on well with her students, but has also experienced challenges related to them. These experiences were the reason for deliberately choosing a school with few problems for her first one-year position. Consequently, it is not surprising that Eva responds by mentioning some critical incidents from the period before her current position. Some of the challenges were related to the fact that some students had a very different background from Eva's. Working among students in the vocational programme, she perceived that she was 'in a foreign world'. Communication is a process of creating something in common (Biesta, 2006). It is therefore easier for teachers to communicate with students with whom the teacher has more in common from the start, a fact the teacher needs to be aware of and must try to compensate for. Every student has the right to be seen and recognised by the teacher. It is not easy to practice fairness and to make a choice between different options. However, even if challenging situations feel uncomfortable, it seems like these situations make teachers reflect and take them further. The teacher has to stop and consider different alternatives. If this happens in a supportive environment, the learning outcome might be great.

The first situation Eva tells about is a very difficult one for a new teacher, namely that of disagreeing with the administration, with her colleagues and with external experts. Here they treated a boy in a way Eva could not support. Powerless in her position as a substitute teacher in a short period engagement, she does not know what to do about it. In her opinion, the boy was treated too harshly. She distinguishes between who the boy is and what he does and does not dramatise his behaviour. Eva wants to do the right thing, and what is right or wrong is an ethical issue. Attitudes toward other people and values are no more the domain of 'experts' than of others, and Eva's opinion therefore should be recognised on the same level as other teachers' opinions. Furthermore, young teachers sometimes have a better connection with young people than more experienced colleagues and might better understand the situation from the student's perspective. On one hand, Eva wants to act in the best interests of the student, but she also wants to be loyal to her colleagues.

Colnerud (2015) claims teachers often act in conflict with their own conscience. They have a double loyalty, towards their students and the institution, and they have a mandate to serve the students as well as society. Sometimes teachers experience conflicts between the different perspectives. In Eva's case, she felt a dilemma between her personal and professional ethic versus the school's decision. As a new teacher, Eva was alone and powerless and felt she could not act on her judgment. Caring is about being aware of the needs of those for whom one is caring. It was here that Eva's moral values were at stake. She wants to protect a pupil from harm. At the same time, she does not want to criticise her colleagues or the administration. The institutional constraints are in conflict with her conscience. We can also assume she wants to protect herself. So what could Eva have done? Teachers need to share dilemmas and talk about them with others (Colnerud, 2015). In a more permanent position, Eva might find someone she could trust and discuss her dilemma with. As it is, the dilemma remains unresolved and put pressure on Eva.

It is not uncommon for new teachers to feel powerless (Thomas & Beauchamp, 2010; Rots, Kelchtermans, & Aelterman, 2012). In this respect, the school culture plays a major role. The first year the teachers find their own way and at the same time are affected by the powerful socializing forces of the school culture (Caspersen & Raaen, 2014). The novice teacher finds it easy to adapt to the culture and do as the others do. It is described as a taboo to criticize a colleague (Colnerud, 2006). By criticising, teachers risk their own safety in their community. Eva is not the first new teacher that feels powerless in the school culture. "Cecilie" from a previous study explains that she felt no right to speak (Smith, Ulvik, & Helleve, 2013). Little by little, she became aware that she was a fully worthy member of the staff, and she started to express herself in meetings. To her surprise, her colleagues actually listened to what she had to say. She concludes that one is allowed to be a newcomer, but that one is also allowed to participate.

The second situation Eva identifies as a critical incident happened in a class where Eva suddenly finds herself in the middle of a situation she does not know how to handle. What is she supposed to do? It is her choice; no one can take it away from her. She has to use what van Manen (1991) calls pedagogical thoughtfulness, or the tact of teaching. It is not always easy to know whether the teacher's interpretation of a situation is adequate. The tact of teaching is a more intuitive way of acting when deliberation and reflection are impossible and an immediate response is demanded. Løsgstrup (1969) writes about demands that are unvoiced and need to be discovered. Being able to discover these demands, one has to be attentive to others.

Consequently, it is not always a straightforward task to perceive and understand students' needs. Sometimes teachers lack resources to meet the needs, other times the teacher might disapprove of the need. Nodding (2012) distinguishes between assumed and expressed needs. The teacher sometimes presume to know what students need. Nodding states that a carer should be attentive and watch and listen. The empathy of care ethics is other-oriented. When Eva does not know how best to act, she decides to discuss the issue with her students. Reflecting in action implies taking a risk (Schön, 1991). Professionals have to make independent decisions, but that does not mean that others should not inform the decisions, whether it be students, colleagues or the literature. However, what Eva decided could have been a problematic decision and it presupposes a positive relationship. What if the teacher and students disagree or a student feels he or she is exposed to discrimination? Being a teacher involves acting without fixed answers or recipes. It should be added that the relationship between students and teachers is more informal in Norway than in other countries, and that most students report a good relationship with their teachers (Wendelborg, Røe, & Caspersen, 2016). Consequently, it might be perceived as more acceptable in Norway than in other countries for teachers to ask students for advice.

While new teachers tend to focus on themselves, Eva has already showed that she has a heart for her students and wants to hear what they have to say. Her previous experiences might have been helpful in that respect. Biesta, Priestley, and Robinson (2015) emphasise the importance of a vision of education. Without a purpose, the possibilities for actions seem limited. This may mean that it is easier for a teacher who knows what she wants to decide what to do, and it will be easier to judge contributions from others. The researchers claim that access to a wider perspective might provide a horizon against which teachers' own beliefs can be evaluated. Eva discussed with her colleagues before reading the short story, and we might assume that she perceived the story to be controversial. Even though she has thought her decision through beforehand, she still finds herself in a dilemma in the class and has to make an in-flight decision. Eva does have some visions. She wants to prioritise vulnerable students, for example. However, as a new teacher it is not easy to act on her view and decide offhand what considerations she should prioritise.

5.3   *Ethical Judgements*

Dealing with the two critical incidents, Eva had to choose among competing considerations and to decide what she considered to be the right action. She had to make what is termed an ethical judgement. Teachers seem to lack a moral vocabulary (Colnerud, 2015). Without a vocabulary, it can be difficult to discuss ethical issues and even to think about ethical judgements. Teachers consider ethics to be important, but find the topic vague and often experience a mismatch between ideal theories and what happens in practice (Schjetne et al., 2016). A group of Norwegian researchers suggest empirical ethics as an alternative to a more theoretical approach, that is, an ethic that begins with what people value and are committed to instead of starting in theory (ibid.). They suggest three steps or approaches: articulation, disturbance and expansion. The first step is descriptive, but also happens in interplay with theory. When people describe a situation, they bring with them previous knowledge. The next step, disturbance, implies that the articulation is thrown off balance. In practice, there are conflicts and tensions and even though people use the phrase "the best for the child", it is not clear what it means. Disturbance might be a result of pressure from a number of stakeholders. However, it might also be an important source for development. The last step, expansion, is a shift from a descriptive to a more normative discussion. A description will always depend on the describer and is therefore incomplete. Thus, one needs to see the situation in a broader perspective and question what is taken for granted.

We do not know if Eva considers her critical incidents as ethical dilemmas, but in both cases, she wants to do what she perceives as right. Using the first critical incident as an example, she *describes* the situation, as called for in the first step of empirical ethics. She evaluates the existing practice as bad. A *disturbing* approach, for example, could be to ask why the other stakeholders act as they do instead of immediately judging their actions as bad. An attempt at understanding their approach might make it easier to reach a broader understanding of the situation, which in turn might have enabled Eva to contribute in a constructive way. *Expanding* the situation could be to move from the micro-situation in the classroom and include the conditions that constitute the local ethical space.

Instead of trying to live up to ideals that seem out of reach, empirical ethics starts in practice and might provide a more realistic approach. Normative theories can be used to analyse situations and to offer a critical perspective. Empirical ethics focuses on ethics in practice, but ethics informed by theories.

6 Conclusion

Eva wants to have a manageable job and takes steps to get it, even if it implies to accept a temporary position rather than a permanent one. Her story shows that it can be useful to have experiences from different schools. She knows, for example that collaboration works differently in different schools. As a newly qualified teacher, Eva experiences some critical incidents that makes her reflect. There are no fixed answers, and she has to choose among competing considerations. In these situations, it is helpful for Eva to have a vision, but she misses colleagues to discuss dilemmas with. Through professional dialogue different perspectives can be revealed and the involved parties might learn from each other, either they are experienced teachers or teachers with a newcomer and outsider perspective.

References

Biesta, G. J. J. (2006). *Beyond learning. Democratic education for a human future*. London: Paradigm Publishers.
Biesta, G. J. J., Priestley, M., & Robinson, S. (2015). The role of beliefs in teacher agency. *Teachers and Teaching: Theory and Practice, 21*(6), 624–640.
Caspersen, J., & Raaen, F. D. (2014). Novice teachers and how they cope. *Teachers and Teaching: Theory and Practice, 20*(2), 189–211.
Colnerud, G. (2006). Teacher ethics as a research problem: Syntheses achieved and new issues. *Teachers and Teaching: Theory and Practice, 12*(3), 365–385.
Colnerud, G. (2015). Moral stress in teaching practice. *Teachers and Teaching: Theory and Practice, 21*(3), 346–360.
Dewey, J. (1933). *How we think*. Boston, MA: D.C. Heath and Company.
Dobber, M., Akkerman, S., Verloop, N., & Vermunt, J. D. (2012). Student teachers' collaborative research: Small scale research projects during teacher education. *Teaching and Teacher Education, 28*, 609–617.
Eisner, E. (2002). From episteme to phronesis to artistry in the study and improvement of teaching. *Teaching and Teacher Education, 18*, 375–385.
Engvik, G. (2014). The importance of networks for newly qualified teachers in upper secondary education. *Educational Research, 56*(4), 453–472.

Flores, M. A., & Day, C. (2006). Contexts which shape and reshape new teachers' identities: A multi-perspective study. *Teaching and Teacher Education, 22*, 219–232.

Hargreaves, A. (1994). *Changing Teachers, changing times: Teachers work and culture in a postmodern age.* London: Cassell.

Løgstrup, K. E. (1969). *Den etiske fordring.* Oslo: Cappelen.

Mansfield, C., Beltman, S., & Price, A. (2014). 'I'm coming back again!' The resilience process of early career teachers. *Teachers and Teaching: Theory and Practice, 20*(5), 547–567.

Nilsson, P. (2009). From lesson plan to new comprehension: Exploring student teachers' pedagogical reasoning in learning about teaching. *European Journal of Teacher Education, 32*(3), 239–258.

Noddings, N. (2012). The caring relation in teaching. *Oxford Review of Education, 38*(6), 771–781.

Penlington, C. (2008). Dialog as a catalyst for teacher change: A conceptual analysis. *Teaching and Teacher Education, 24*(5), 1304–1316.

Rippon, J., & Martin, M. (2006). Call me teacher: The quest of new teachers. *Teachers and Teaching: Theory and Practice, 12*(3), 305–324.

Rots, I., Kelchtermans, G., & Aelterman, A. (2012). Learning (not) to become a teacher: A qualitative analyses of the job entrance issue. *Teaching and Teacher Education, 28*, 1–10.

Schjetne, E., Afdal, H. W., Anker, T., Johannesen, N., & Afdal, G. (2016). Empirical moral philosophy and teacher education. *Ethics and Education, 11*(1), 29–41.

Schön, D. A. (1991). *The reflective practitioner. How professionals think in action.* Aldershot: Avebury.

Smith, K., Ulvik, M., & Helleve, I. (2013). *Førstereisen – Lærdom hentet fra nye læreres fortellinger* [First journey – Lessons learned from novice teachers]. Oslo: Gyldendal.

Thomas, L., & Beauchamp, C. (2011). Understanding new teachers' professional identities through metaphor. *Teaching and Teacher Education, 27*, 762–769.

Tripp, D. (1994). Teachers' lives, critical incidents, and professional practice. *Qualitative Studies in Education, 7*(1), 65–76.

Ulvik, M., & Langørgen, K. (2012). What is there to learn from a new teacher? Newly qualified teachers as a resource in schools. *Teachers and Teaching: Theory and Practice, 18*(1), 43–57.

Van Eekelen, I. M., Vermunt, J. D., & Boshuizen, H. P. A. (2006). Exploring teachers' will to learn. *Teaching and Teacher Education, 22*, 408–423.

Van Manen, M. (1991). *The tact of teaching: The meaning of pedagogical thoughtfulness.* Albany, NY: State University of New York Press.

Wendelborg, C., Røe, M., & Caspersen, J. (2016). *Elevundersøkelsen 2015 – hovedrapporten.* Retrieved from https://www.udir.no/tall-og-forskning/finn-forskning/rapporter/elevundersokelsen-2015--hovedrapporten/

PART 6

Conclusions

CHAPTER 12

Lessons Learned from the Teachers' Stories

1   Introduction

When reading the stories from the five different countries, Australia, England, Finland, Israel and Norway, our first impression was optimism. The stories tell about competent, enthusiastic, highly motivated and resilient teachers at the very beginning of their career. This seems to us to contradict much for the rather negative literature about novice teachers and the many challenges they meet in the first year. We hear much about attrition from teaching, and the high numbers reported in several studies from various places are certainly alarming (Schaeffer, Long, & Clandinin, 2012; Tiplic, Brandmo, & Elstad, 2015). Indeed, the novice teachers tell about difficulties, they are honest about wanting to give up, but they also seem to be sufficiently resilient to meet the various challenges drawing on self-efficacy, motivation, support, and not least, drawing on the relationships they develop with students. All the 10 teachers we met through this book are looking into the future with intentions of staying in teaching, practicing the profession for which they were educated. The stories suggest that there is another side to being a novice teacher than what is most commonly told (Ulvik, Smith, & Helleve, 2009).

In this last chapter, we want to present some of the lessons we have learned from listening to the novice teachers' stories. The main issues discussed were agreed upon after the three of us first had read all the texts individually, before having intense and enriching discussions about what we learned from the stories. Guided by the literature presented in the first chapter, and by the interview guide that was used to elicit the narratives, we decided to focus on motivation, expectations and reality, on-job learning, relations, and mentoring/support.

The structure of the chapter is that we present the findings from each country before highlighting similarities and differences from the various contexts. A summary of the above five categories are presented according to countries in a table before drawing some horizontal conclusions. As we see it, this will enable us to conclude with lessons learned which might be relevant across national contexts. Caution should be taken, however, that the stories represent two teachers from each of the five countries, and they cannot be representative for generalisability purposes.

2 Motivation

2.1 *Australia*

The two teachers from Australia share a deep devotion for their job as teachers. They have both grown up with parents who are either teachers or pre-school teachers. Eric has loved to join his mother in her work in the kindergarten while Carol was kind of "born" into teaching since her parents met in teacher education. She has loved to teach others ever since she was a small child. Her passion is closely connected to helping and supporting others in their learning and development process. In her opinion teaching is too fun to be a real job. And actually that's exactly the same with Eric. When he is watching young people he wishes he could influence their lives. Both the Australian teachers know that their parents' attitude to teaching has influenced them. They also know that their parents wanted them to become teachers. However, it is also important for them to underline that the decision to become teachers is their own choice. In fact both of them have purposefully tried to do something else than teaching, but soon landed on the conclusion that teaching was their profession. These two Australian teachers seem to be intrinsically motivated wanting to teach as well as wanting to influence young people's lives, which is a kind of altruistic motivation. Teaching has been in the family for both.

2.2 *England*

The English teachers, Anna and Owen are intrinsically motivated. They had other jobs before starting on a Post Graduate Certificate in Education (PGCE) programme, but they both decided to become teachers because they love their subjects and want to work with young people. "I am not an office person", Anna claims, and Owen underlines how creative the teaching profession is. He enjoys planning and to be together with students. The two of them also emphasise the caring dimension and thereby reveal an altruistic motivation. None of them mention teachers in their families, but Owen refers to his own good school experiences with inspiring teachers.

Even if Anna and Owen initially wanted to go into teaching because they wanted to pass on their subjects, they seem to be very connected to their students and their well-being.

2.3 *Finland*

The Finnish teachers have a quite different approach to the profession than many other teachers in this book. None of them has parents or close relatives who are teachers. No other persons seem to have influenced their choices. It is a personal decision. For Alice the idea came when she was a teenager. For Maria as well the idea came gradually as she was getting older. However, they both seem to share the idea that teaching is an important profession. Both teachers underline that teaching is a high status profession in Finland. Alice describes how difficult it is to be admitted to teacher education, especially in the Swedish speaking part of Finland. A written application is not enough. She also had to write an essay and to go through an interview. She did not succeed the first year and had to apply again the next. Maria tells that it is difficult to get a job as a teacher. The Finnish teachers value the high status which might indicate a kind of extrinsic motivation in their choice of profession, however, this is combined with a more social utility motive, believing teaching is important for the society.

2.4 Israel

Aviva, who is a special education teacher, feels strongly about wanting to help children who are less fortunate, and she beliefs that helping these children to succeed is important for the society as well. Thus, she reflects strong altruistic and social value motifs in her story. She has chosen her profession mainly for idealistic reasons, and cares less about the status and the salary. Yael expresses a strong intrinsic motivation as she emphasises the importance of enjoying geography and teaching it to young people. However, she also finds geography important to teach the young generation about how to protect the environment. This indicates social utility motivation for choosing to become a teacher. In the Israeli sample, the type of motivation held seems to be reflected in the age group and discipline taught in school.

2.5 Norway

Endre and Eva both want to make a difference in students' lives. Endre has many teachers in his family, and eventually he decided to become a teacher himself. During teacher education he was not sure that he would manage. However, as a qualified teacher he experiences that teaching offers joy and fulfilment. He looks forward to going to work every day. Especially he enjoys contact with students and thinks he is good at establishing relationships with them. He feels sorry for students who are let down, and he is willing to make an extra effort for them. His motivation can be characterized as intrinsic and altruistic. Eva's parents are teachers, and also Eva considers teaching as the best choice of profession for her. She enjoys teaching and cannot think of anything better to do and want to be there for her students, similar to Endre.

3 Expectations and Reality

3.1 *Australia*

The first period for the Australian teachers is characterized as different from anything else they had experienced. Two aspects seem to be typical for the start of their career. First, it is an overwhelming period because there are many different tasks they have to handle for which they are not prepared. Second, when looking back, they can see that they did things very elaborately.

They met many new colleagues with whom they had to establish relations. They were newcomers in an organization and had the position of the newcomer. They felt insecure about the main rules for conduct, and practical things such as where to find material and equipment.

In retrospect, the newly qualified teachers said they spent a lot more time than they needed on different activities and tasks. Doing things for the first time without experience takes time. The planning took more time than necessary and as Eric said "There was a lot of repeating myself and going over things I had done, and what was the best way of doing things?" However, the Australian teachers are both satisfied with their own way of handling the first six months of their job when they look back.

3.2 *England*

The workload seems to be more extensive than expected for the English teachers, and they both work long hours. However, the transition phase does not seem like a shock. May be it is less shocking for those who have teaching as a second career, and also who have some standards that might work as guidelines. Owen describes that the pressure is something he learned about during pre-service teacher education. They both have their ups and downs, and for Anna being a new teacher is like being on a roller-coaster. However, she tells that she experiences mostly ups.

3.3 *Finland*

When it comes to the Finnish teachers, Maria did not mention the first period specifically, while Alice described it as a period when she was so anxious and nervous that she had forgotten most of what happened. She seems to have been thrown into a difficult class-situation where she was left to herself to solve the problems. Apparently, she had expected to spend time on teaching the subject, but instead she realizes that most of her time is spent on educational issues not related to the subject matter. Clearly there is a gap between practice and reality for Alice during her first months as a teacher. However, when she realized that there was a bullying-team that could help her and the pupils, she is relieved. What seems to be missing is information about where she could get support. Alice tried a lot of different solutions before she asked one of her colleagues who told her about the team.

3.4 Israel

Aviva, who was working with young children in special education had not expected the many tasks that had little to do with teaching, such as making sure the children were eating or that they could put on their back packs at the end of the day. Teacher education had certainly not prepared her for how to handle parents who quarrelled about what was best for their child in parents' meetings. "Theories about education and special education had not prepared me for these situations, and the famous, or notorious theory – practice gap was right there, straight in my face". Yael, working with older children was not fully ready for handling the many discipline problems she experienced in the beginning, and part of it was the lack of motivation students showed for her favourite subject, geography. However, when she succeeded in getting the students interested in her subject, the success really motivated her to continue teaching.

3.5 Norway

Both Endre and Eva knew that it would be hectic the first year. However, they were not prepared for issues outside the classroom. Endre thinks that the first months in the school could have been better organized and include more basic information. Teacher education could have prepared him better for making lesson plans for example. He has a feeling of reinventing the wheel all the time. Furthermore, he has to teach his minor subject with which he did not feel fully confident, and he had to take over a challenging class in the middle of the year. Still he describes his first year as okay. One reason for that can be that he is not afraid of failing, something he learned from his practicum.

Eva has a busy life outside school, and as a consequence teaching has not taken over her life as she sees it. She knows that teaching is busy and has taken actions to prevent that the job will be too hard – not a full time job, and in a "good" school. What she had not expected, however, was the limited cooperation among her colleagues. She knows from her practice schools that it can be otherwise.

4 On-Job Learning

4.1 Australia

Carol and Eric both report that they think they have been very lucky with the colleagues in their schools. According to Eric there is so much stuff you have to learn on the job while you are teaching. They are included in a community of practice where they are well taken care of. They are both parts of teams that have regular meeting-points and describe the team-work they experience as better than anything else compared to other teachers in the present school, or compared to other newly qualified teachers they know from the university. Apparently, it means a lot to have colleagues who are flexible and help the newcomer to seek solutions instead of focusing on the problems. According to Eric, the best way to go forward and learn as a teacher is to ask whenever necessary. Teaching is contextual and the questions that come up are connected to the specific situation in which the new teachers find themselves. Having the possibility to ask somebody with more experience when the question is urgent seems to be crucial for the Australian teachers.

4.2   England

During the first year Anna and Owen had to find their way as teachers and to learn to deal with the workload. What Anna found hard was to plan her teaching from scratch, while other teachers had something on which to build. She also found behaviour management challenging and realised this was something she had to improve. Owen pointed at assessment as something he was not trained in and found time-consuming. In England there are standards for teaching that direct much of their on-job learning (Department of Education, 2013).

4.3   Finland

The Finnish teachers did not mention their colleagues to the same extent as their Australian colleagues, for example, when it comes to on-job learning. Maria appreciates the open atmosphere among her colleagues and the possibility she has to ask if there is something she is uncertain about. However, there does not seem to be any fixed meeting-points earmarked for mutual learning or team-work among the teachers. The teachers' autonomy is underlined. Maria described how she gradually received respect from students and developed relationship through deliberately showing her students respect. She also tried to make her personal ethical conduct explicit. Based on the two stories from Finland it may seem that the teachers are more left on their own than the Australian teachers. Alice describes her first two years as a kind of psychological roller coaster. Except for the support she gets from the mentoring system outside her own school, she has to struggle with her problems on her own.

4.4   Israel

Aviva was on the verge of giving up teaching in the middle of the first year, after having been bullied by a student in the school yard. However, instead of just giving up, she learned about herself that she was strong enough to learn from the incident and she became more confident in her job. Yael had a similar experience with one of her most difficult students, and she learned that instead of keeping on blaming him and shouting at him, she could show him an empathetic side and strengthen his self-concept. When this proved successful, she learned that constantly being angry with difficult students does not solve the problem. Both Israeli teachers learned about how to work with demanding students and class management.

4.5   Norway

The transition from student to work life is for the two Norwegian teachers a big change in their life. Starting to work implies for Endre to get into a circadian rhythm. He feels like a real grown up, and Eva says something similar in her interview. The first thing Endre had to learn at the workplace was how to teach a subject he had not been prepared for in teacher education. Furthermore, he had to find out different practical issues by himself, and learn to deal with students with diverse needs. He had to ask for information and sees it as his responsibility to ask for it. Eva, on her side, experiences some situations where there are no clear cut answers. She learned that it is possible to discuss difficult decisions with students and to learn from them.

5   Relations

5.1   Australia

For many newly qualified teachers positive experiences in building relations to students and classes seem to be crucial for their self-understanding as teachers. Eric and Alice from Australia are no exceptions. What really makes it worth working as a teacher is to get the satisfaction of seeing students succeed in their learning-process. When the two Australian teachers were asked if they had any experience from the first year that has made an impression on them, they do not hesitate to answer. They both claim that these incidents have changed their view of themselves as teachers. It is as if the experience has asserted them that they are real teachers who are able to manage on their own. The episode Eric mentions is that he got an advice from an experienced teacher. This teacher told him that the best he could do was to let the boy leave the room. He decides to act differently from the advice. For Eric and the boy this turns out to be the right decision. Carol has the same kind of experience with a boy who was about to leave the school when she took over the class. She changed the situation for the boy, and his parents are very grateful. Like Eric, she also manages a situation in spite of an experienced teacher's advice. Both describe the situation as a kind of turning-point where they saw themselves as real teachers who were able to take their own decisions and succeed.

5.2   *England*

Relationships with pupils are central for Anna and Owen as for many newly qualified teachers. Anna enjoys teaching and to be with students, but also finds it challenging. She experiences that one of her students dislikes her. However, she does not have to handle the situation by herself, and is told that the girl dislikes everyone. Furthermore, when some of her students start fighting, she is told that she should not take it personal. In the end, the good experiences outweigh the negative. Owen finds it rewarding to be with students. He experiences it as challenging, however, if they do not want to learn, and describes it as amazing when students leave the classroom happily.

5.3   *Finland*

Alice tells about a critical incident as a positive turning-point in her relation with students, and like many other teachers in this book, it is connected to a concrete episode. In her case there was a boy who had a bad and unpredictable behavior when he became angry. She was also given advice from experienced teachers, e.g. that she should let him go because there was no other possibility. Anyway, she decided to talk with the boy while he was calm. They made a deal that turned out to be the solution and the end of the problem. For Alice this is important for her self-understanding and self-respect as a teacher. Maria had no concrete incident to refer to. From she started as a teacher she seems to have been aware of the fact that working systematically with gaining respect from the pupils would help her to establish positive relations.

5.4   *Israel*

Aviva was surprised to learn that many students have a negative attitude to teachers in general, and she decided she wanted to change that, and worked deliberately by approaching students, not only her own, with respect. Seeing the individual child, especially in her special education class was important to Aviva, and she became attached to and motivated by good relations with students. Yael also acted according to her own intuition and values, when she started to give one of the most difficult students' responsibilities, such as finding relevant material on you-tube. Little by little mutual trust was developed. She felt that at the end of the year, it became an emotional burden to leave the class with which she had worked so hard to develop good relations. At the same time it also gave her lots of motivation to continue teaching.

5.5 Norway

Both Norwegian teachers want to make a difference in students' lives. Endre finds that his relationship with student is very good. He learns their names quickly and he also assumes that he, as a tall and strong man, would get some natural authority. He does not have the role of a home room teacher the first year and thinks it is good not to have that responsibility. Eva wants her students to think independently and to listen to them. She believes that students have something to offer. A positive relationship with students is for Endre and Eva part of the motivation for going into teaching in the first place, and they both seem to keep their motivation.

6 Mentoring/Support

6.1 Australia

The newly qualified teachers we meet from Australia are very satisfied with the way they are supported. The school has a mentor-programme caring for support on different levels. On the first level they have the opportunity to collaborate with other newcomers in the same school. Carol and her newly qualified colleague are working very closely; actually they have a glass-door between their classrooms. They are observing and mentoring each other. Another part of the programme ensures that the group of newly qualified teachers can meet regularly and discuss common challenges. Then each pair of newcomers shares a mentor with five years' experience. The assistant principal is also involved in mentoring as the leader of a mentoring system which seems to be very well organized and appreciated by the newly qualified teachers. The way mentoring is organized seems to involve novice as well as experienced teachers. In Carol's understanding the school's policy is to give newly engaged teachers a lot of support in the beginning to secure a safe start of their career. She describes her school as a learning community where also experienced teachers are involved in mentoring groups. This system may not be the same all over Australia; however, it seems to be a very important support for these two and a mentoring system that other schools could learn from.

6.2 England

Both Anna and Owen experience their colleagues as supportive. Interestingly, Anna tells that her colleagues are very helpful, and she assumes this is because she does not work in a prestige school with competition among colleagues. Implicitly she says that standards might promote competition and a climate with less sharing. Furthermore, they have both been assigned a mentor and are assessed according to the standards. However, the support is experienced as very different for the two. Both are supposed to have regular meetings with their mentors. However, Anna's mentor is busy and does not have time to follow up the mentees, while Owen describes the mentor arrangement in his school as excellent with frequent meetings. Compared to other new teachers in this book, the English teachers get more help and in some ways are given recipes for, or are told, how to act.

6.3   Finland

The Finnish teachers are part of the national mentor-system Osaava Verme (Aspfors & Hansén, 2011). This means that they meet regularly every month with other newly qualified teachers. These meetings, which are highly appreciated by the novices, are led by an experienced teacher who is mentoring the group. In the meetings they discuss issues with which they are concerned. In their own school, they have regular meetings with their principal, and they also have an appointed mentor who can answer questions and give them support. The support they get inside school is individual and not part of the rest of the school organization. Collaborative support tends to take place outside the school when they meet other newly qualified teachers from other schools. To a very little extent our Finnish teachers speak about their colleagues. This may be accidental for these two teachers and not typical for other schools in Finland. However, as referred to by Professor Sven-Erik Hansèn in this book, Finland emphasises a high level of teacher autonomy. According to Maria she has no fixed time when she has to be present except for a meeting every other week. To a large extent she chooses the curriculum herself. Alice does not mention colleagues at all except for the group-meetings in Osaava Verme.

6.4   Israel

Aviva felt she was supported all though her first year as she never felt alone. Aviva appreciated the fact she had someone to turn to when things got tough. Yael tells about similar experiences and she adds that she did not only have a designated mentor to whom 'she talked and talked' but she also felt supported by the whole school, including the principal. This suggests that a culture of support to novice teachers in Israel have been developed as mentoring in Israel is well incorporated at the systemic level for more than a decade.

6.5   Norway

Both Endre and Eva are given full responsibility from the first day. Endre has a mentor, but not from the start when he needs it the most. He understands why there is attrition in teaching. His colleagues are friendly, but busy, and the cooperation could have been better. Eva is frustrated because there is not much cooperation at work. There is sharing, but not cooperation. Many colleagues follow the plans as they are used to and are not interesting in doing things in new ways.

7 The Future

7.1 Australia

The two Australian teachers are devoted to their profession from they were very young. They have never doubted the choice of becoming teachers and they never seem to doubt if they are going to continue as teachers. Carol is looking forward to next year when the routines are known and she knows the staff. She has learnt the lesson that she is going to have high expectations to the pupils from the beginning. Eric is also optimistic based on the experiences he has gained the first year. He is always reflecting on his job and he loves to do it. He claims that making mistakes is no problem because he can learn from it. His worry is if he and his newly educated colleagues are able to get a job. He describes how the system is a worry that occupies much of their concentration the last month of spring every year, until they become what he calls "ongoing" which means having a permanent job. Until they get this ongoing-certificate they have to repeatedly apply for their jobs and go through the interview process. Carol on the other hand has got a permanent job and does not mention the application process at all.

7.2 England

Anna is optimistic when she thinks about the future. The job is busy, but she thinks next year will be better and that she will improve when it comes to behaviour management. She also mentions that in England it is possible for teachers to be promoted and have a career. Owen would like to be head of department. None of the other teachers in the book talk about promotions. However, Owen points at the policy in education in England, and he does not want to stay in teaching if the school increases the focus on assessment driven by targets. New teachers tend to focus on the school level, but Owen, as well as Endre in Norway, refers to policy decisions that might affect their decisions about whether to continue teaching. Both Anna and Owen are in their probationer year and might fail. However, they do not seem to worry about their future jobs. Most newly qualified pass the first year, and they seem to think they will be in that group. They both got their jobs in competition with others, and Owen, who was offered a job in his practice school, tells that he enjoys the school and thinks they like him as well.

7.3 Finland

The two teachers from Finland seem to have a different approach when it comes to decisions if to stay in the profession. While Maria has a steady course from the beginning and never seems to doubt if she has chosen the right profession, Alice has her ups and downs during the first four semesters as a newly qualified teacher. Finally, when she returned to the forth semester she was sure that she wanted to stay in the profession as a teacher. Apparently she has struggled with herself during this period of one and a half years. She has not been on sick leave, and she has not dropped out, but two of her semesters were really tough. During the first semester she was so anxious that she cannot remember much. When she came back after summer vacation she also had a hard autumn. She experienced the class to be difficult and her reaction was to become irritated. The end of the third semester was a critical moment in Maria's decision to stay in the profession or to leave. She blames herself for not being a good enough teacher. What she admitted and learnt from the others in the mentor group, is that she had to accept that if she was staying she had to realize that she could not save every pupil.

Alice thinks that because of the experiences she had during the different crisis she went through, the forth semester is going to be exciting. She has energy and is able to laugh with the pupils instead of becoming irritated. At the moment she is more relaxed than she used to be. Maria is also optimistic when it comes to future expectations.

7.4 Israel

Aviva knows she wants to stay in education, not necessarily teaching, but to work within the educational system. She does not explain this by talking negatively about teaching, on the contrary. It is more a career development for her, and as a teacher the career ladder in Israel is rather narrow. A similar view is expressed by Yael in her story. She is happy with the first year and feels she learned a lot about herself and about teaching. In the far future she might want to share her experiences with new teachers, so she is also indicating a career development which might take her out of the classroom, but within education.

7.5 Norway

Endre wants to continue in teaching, however, not if the working hours for teachers are changed in a wrong direction. He looks forward to the second year and will make more long-term-plans and improve the cooperation with others. Also Eva wants to continue as a teacher, and wants to improve how to provide better for vulnerable students. Their first year in teaching has had its ups and downs, but in the end it turns out that the positive experiences are dominating, and what motivated them to teach, is still alive. A problematic issue that stresses Endre is that he does not know if he has a job the next year. With a lot to do at the end of the year, he also has to apply for a new job. Contrary to Eva, he is educated in subjects that are not that common in school and it might be difficult to get a job in – at least in urban areas.

8 Discussion

In this section we will discuss the above table in a horizontal manner, relating to literature we have found relevant to the issues discussed.

8.1 *Motivation*

Watt, Richardson, and Smith (2017) claim that motivation for teaching will vary depending on the context in which teaching is practiced, such as national frameworks, salaries, status of the profession, etc. However, at the same time the above authors also state that international research shows that in spite of the contextual differences, the desire to teach is driven by "a desire to undertake meaningful work that makes for a better, more equitable society; they also want to work with children/adolescents and, importantly, believe they possess the abilities needed to teach" (Watt, Richardson, & Smith, 2017, p. 5). This aligns, to a large extent, with the stories told by the novice teachers we have interviewed for this book. It seems that the younger the students are, the stronger the altruistic motifs for teaching, and for teachers working with older children, a genuine wish to make others interested in the subject taught, seems to be prevalent (Nesje, Brandmo, & Berger, 2018). Incentives such as salaries and high status are not among the strongest motifs for choosing teaching as a professional career (OECD, 2005; Watt, Richardson, & Smith, 2017), a claim that is confirmed by 'our' new teachers. Having said that, the Finnish teachers expressed satisfaction with the high status teaching has in their country.

However, in a large Australian study among novice teachers Richardson and Watt (2016) found that newly educated teachers acknowledged the low status of their profession, the heavy workload and emotional demands. Surprisingly, they still expressed a high degree of satisfaction for teaching as a professional career, and their initial intrinsic and altruistic motifs for teaching were sustained. The stories in this book tell about hard work, demanding challenges, and critical incidents. Yet, all of the participants say they want to continue teaching, at least in the near future.

The main reason for the strong resilience seems to be the confidence in their own abilities to teach, their self-efficacy, as confirmed by Nesje, Brandmo, and

TABLE 12.1 Summary of findings

Country	Motivation	Expectations	On-job learning	Relations students	Mentoring/support	Future
Australia	Intrinsic/altruistic/teachers in the family	Unprepared for handling not teaching related tasks/micro-politics/time-consuming	Ask for help/not be afraid to be new	Acting on intuition and personal/values	Happy with support/support system/peer support	Continue teaching/positive experiences/motivated/worry about job situation
England	Intrinsic/altruistic/no teachers in the family	More work than expected/no real practice shock	How to manage workload/classroom management/standards	Not taking bullying 'disliking' personal/rewarding to be with students	Supportive colleagues/named mentor – different quality of mentoring/told what to do	Continue teaching/positive experiences/stressed by target driven teaching/positive about job situation
Finland	No teachers in the family/high status/social utility	Unprepared for handling not teaching related tasks/missing information about support	To be autonomous/individual learning/learn to be on your own	Turning point when solving a critical issue/acting on intuition and personal values/establishing trust	Group mentoring/individual mentoring/not much collegial support	Continue teaching in spite of struggle/supported by mentor/optimistic view of future

(*cont.*)

TABLE 12.1 Summary of findings (*cont.*)

Country	Motivation	Expectations	On-job learning	Relations students	Mentoring/support	Future
Israel	Altruistic/social utility/intrinsic-age and subject dependent	Unprepared for handling not teaching related tasks/discipline/class-management	Develop empathy for students/classroom management based on mutual respect	Seeing the individual student/acting on intuition and personal values/difficult to leave a class	Happy with support/support system/whole school support including principal	Stay in education, not necessarily in the classroom/narrow career ladder/happy with first year
Norway	Intrinsic/altruistic (teachers in the family)	Unprepared for handling not teaching related tasks/out of field teaching/time-consuming/lack of cooperation	Content knowledge due to out-of-field teaching/handling diversity/class-management/listen to and talk to students	Strong male authority/learning names/listening to students/good relations motivate	Friendly colleagues/little cooperation, some sharing/little mentioning of mentoring	Conscious decision to continue/worry about job situation
Conclusions	Similar motifs, high status in Finland; not salary related	Similar to all: Unprepared for handling not teaching related tasks/time-consuming/Norway lack of collegial cooperation/Israel discipline issues	Learned about classroom-management across three countries/develop mutual trust and respect/Finland becoming independent	Similarities: Acting on intuition and personal values/motivation from good relations	Diverse responses as regards support	Similar to all: continue teaching or in education/insecure job situation for some/pleased with first year

Berger (2018) in a recent Norwegian study. The stories tell that the confidence as a teacher is strengthened after successfully meeting challenges, especially with difficult students. From the literature we know that a close relationship with the students is crucial the first year in teaching (Aspfors & Bondas, 2013; Flores, 2006).

The strong altruistic and intrinsic motifs for teaching are vulnerable when looking at staying in the profession throughout the career. Many educational systems are undergoing repeated reforms, there are increasing demands of documentation and accountability framed by overarching national regulations (Richardson & Watt, 2016). This is a threat to teachers' professional autonomy and the opportunities to enact professional agency. Morgan et al. (2010) claim that it is how new teachers perceive events at a micro level that most strongly impact their motivation and learning. We argue that macro politics, such as national frameworks and regulations which de-professionalize teachers, are equally central to sustaining motivation for teaching. To keep teachers' motivation it is crucial that they are able to maintain the motivation that brought them to teaching in the first place and that there is a frequency of positive events (ibid.). Furthermore, it is important that there is no mismatch between idealistic motivation and the reality they face (Johnsen et al., 2014).

9   Expectations and Reality

The transition from being taught to teaching others is often characterised as a practice shock. This is a well-known concept in the research literature and refers to a discrepancy between the ideal perception of teaching and reality new teachers may experience (Dicke, Elling, Schmeck, & Leutner, 2015). The teachers in this book expected that teaching would be busy, but not as overwhelming as it actually turned out to be. The workload was heavier than imagined, and they had to work long hours. It took time to do things for the first time without experiences. What really gave some of them a hard time was challenging classes, assignments they were not prepared for, and tasks that had little to do with teaching, like dealing with out of class situations and handling parents.

The entrance into teaching implies an encounter both with performative and organisational aspects of the teaching role (Hermansen, Lorentzen, Mausethagen, & Zlatanovic, 2018). Research on newly qualified teachers often focuses on the performative aspects. However, the entrance into teaching is also about becoming a member of an organisation and establish relations with colleagues. There are rules, routines and practical matters that presuppose information. The school as organisation is characterised by traditions, relationships, structures and values established within the school (Dalin & Kitson, 2004). Every school is different and it often takes time for newcomers to get to know the organisation they have become part of. This was the case for teachers who were left alone in schools with limited cooperation, as experienced by the Norwegian teachers.

Even if all the ten teachers we talked to found teaching demanding, not all of them perceived the entrance into teaching as a shock. In order to reduce the practice shock, the literature points to induction programmes and mentoring (Le Maistre & Pare, 2010; Alhija & Fresko, 2010). Peer-support is suggested, and above all to be given a mentor (Ingersoll & Strong, 2011). The Australian teachers and Owen in England were supported in ways that likely reduced the entrance shock. The Israeli teachers had demanding challenges related to discipline problems and unexpected assignments. However, being supported during the entrance phase became for them an important learning stage (Fresko & Alhija, 2009). The Finnish and Norwegian teachers were left more or less on their own. The Finnish teachers had some support outside the school. However, to be included in the school as an organisation it is also important to be supported in becoming familiar with the school culture.

As we see it, some of the issues related to the gap between expectations and reality can be prepared for during teacher education. Being a teacher implies more than teaching a subject. Both Owen from England and Endre from Norway refer to teacher education as helpful when it comes to understand their future role. However, there are issues that can only be learned at the specific work place, and consequently new teachers should be offered time and opportunities for this learning to take place.

9.1   On Job Learning

One of our student teachers once wrote in the text for her final exam: "It is not until the moment you meet the pupils that you become a teacher". Suppose she was right. Maybe new teachers have to go through the first chaotic months as a newly qualified teacher before they really become certain about their professional choice. Success in building relations to pupils and parents seems to be a crucial aspect. While many other professions gradually increase the responsibilities for newly educated employees, teachers have to take the full responsibility from their first day in school (Aspfors & Bondas, 2013). In the transition from student teacher to qualified teacher a set of coping strategies, according to a survival orientation, to adapt to the new tasks and roles that are required (Flores, 2006; Kyriacou & Kunc, 2007). Our teachers are no exception. However, Kelchtermans and Ballett (2002) point out that an often neglected field is the "political learning" that takes place especially in the first phase of teachers' careers. What is called *micropolitical action is defined as those actions that aim at establishing, safeguarding or restoring the desired working conditions* (p. 108). Throughout the first year the teachers we interviewed tried to develop micropolitical literacy, understood as the competence to understand the issues of power and interests in schools. Three aspects are intertwined in this literacy; the knowledge aspect, an operational and an experimental aspect. The knowledge aspect refers to the knowledge that is needed in order to interpret and understand the micropolitical character of a particular situation, while the operational aspect refers to the teacher's capacity to be able to influence the situation. Finally, the experimental part of the literacy is related to the degree of satisfaction the teacher experiences with his or her own literacy (ibid.). Our informants seem to be satisfied with the position they have gained in their schools. More than anything else classroom management and the success in building relations to pupils seem to be the main instrument for how the teachers judge their own literacy as teachers. Other studies have also found that teachers view good relationships with pupils to be the most satisfying aspect of their work (Nias, 1996; Flores & Day, 2006; Hobson, Malderez, Tracey, Homer, Mitchell, Biddulph, Giannakaki, Rose, Pell, Roper, Chambers, & Tomlinson, 2007; Ulvik, Smith, & Helleve, 2009; Smith, Ulvik, & Helleve, 2013). So was also the case with our teachers.

Micropolitical literacy is developed in collaboration with colleagues. In the conglomerate of human beings inside a school organization the newly qualified teacher has to find her place. On the whole, the majority of our informants are happy with their colleagues, and our impression is that many feel they have been lucky with their colleagues who are described as friendly, but busy.

10   Relations

Teaching is not only a technical or cognitive practice, but also social. However, there has been less attention given to the relational, emotional and caring aspects of teaching (Aspfors & Bondas, 2013). For the teachers in this book these aspects are central. Relationships with pupils seem to be the most essential in new teachers' work (ibid.). Newly qualified teachers want to make a difference in students' lives, and negative relationship is one of the most negative experiences they can have. The ten teachers in our sample fit into this pattern. Their motivation for teaching is closely connected to the relationship they establish with the students. Furthermore, building positive relationships seem to be crucial for their self-understanding as teachers.

What they enjoy most in their work is the contact with students. They want them to succeed and walk happily out of the classroom. However, they all experience challenging situations related to students. Some students have a negative attitude and even dislike the new teacher, and some do not want to learn. There are ups and downs, and all the critical incidents that came up, were connected to students. In the end, the positive experiences outweighed the negative. It means a lot to the teachers to be able to handle challenges with students – especially when they chose to follow their own intuition and values, and make independent decisions, and it works well. Some of them explain how they deliberately try to promote a good relationship, like approaching students with respect, learn their names quickly, and listen to them.

Relationships define new teachers' first work experiences (Aspfors & Bondas, 2013) and consequently it means a lot to them how they manage their classes and are included in the teaching staff. In this book we find examples of challenges among new teachers that can be hard handle even for experienced teachers, like difficult classes or students with special needs. We know from the literature that new teachers often are given challenging classes (Fresko & Alhija, 2009). Furthermore, some of the new teachers experienced limited cooperation among colleagues and had to manage the challenges more or less by themselves.

Despite challenges and a heavy workload, the motivation that brought the teachers to the profession seems to be kept. A reason for that can be that they, after all, developed a positive relationship with their students, and that they met friendly colleagues.

10.1 *Mentoring and Support*

Negative relationships with colleagues are one of the most negative experiences for newly qualified teachers (Aspfors & Bondas, 2013). For novice teachers good collaboration with positive colleagues contributes to make their work more manageable. While our informants on the whole are satisfied with their colleagues and the informal support they get from them, the conditions for formal support differ a lot. Among our informants from the five different countries, we met the whole range of experiences, from a kind of layer on layer mentoring in Australia to no organized mentoring in Norway. Newly qualified teachers in all the countries, except Norway, were introduced to an appointed mentor.

However, mentoring in itself is no guarantee for good mentoring (Hobson, Ashby, Malderez, & Tomlinson, 2009). Maynyard and Furlong (1993) refer to three different mentoring models; the apprentice model, the competence model, and the reflection model. In the *apprentice* perspective the mentor is looked upon as a model for the novice teacher. The *competence* model refers to standards and how the mentor can support the newly qualified teacher in reaching required goals. According to the *reflection* model the mentor is a critical friend; a person who asks provocative questions, provides data to be examined through another lens, and offers critique of a person's work as a friend (Schuck & Russell, 2005).

Mentoring is traditionally a hierarchical and individual activity. Anna, in our book, seems to work within the apprentice and competence model. She tells about her experiences with eight standards that she is going to fulfill and the mentor's role is to just tick off that she fulfills them or not. In order to keep her job she has to meet the standards. While many of our informants refer to a one-to-one mentoring, a number of studies show that peer-group mentoring can be an important means for supporting teachers' professional learning (Heikkinen et al., 2012). In Finland Maria and Alice speak warmly about the Osavva Verme (Kemmis, Heikkinen, Fransson, Aspfors, & Edwards-Groves, 2014) which gave them the opportunity to collaborate with other newly qualified teachers from other schools. They met in groups and had the possibility to discuss common challenges with an experienced mentor. For Alice these meetings probably saved her from attrition. However, the meetings they have with other newly qualified teachers are not part of their own school community, as it is for Carol and Eric in the Australian context. In addition to meetings with other novice teachers, they also meet in groups with more experienced teachers in their school. Hargreaves and Fullan (2000) claim that mentoring needs to be transformed from something that takes place in pairs to an integral part of the school culture, from hierarchical dispensations of wisdom to shared inquiries into practice in order to form strong relationships between experienced and newly qualified colleagues.

10.2   *Future*

All participating teachers in this book ended their stories by being positive to continuing in the profession after the first year. This is positive news and to a certain extent in contradiction to a large body of research that documents high attrition rates among novice teachers (Tiplic, Brandmo, & Elstad, 2015; Harfitt, 2015). The main reasons for drop out are found to be issues related to practice for which the novice teachers were unprepared. Certainly, the stories in this book tell about teachers experiencing being care takers, counsellors, having to deal with situations beyond the curriculum and the classroom. However, instead of this producing a negative attitude, or perceived lack of competence, and intentions of leaving the profession, it seems that as regards the novice teachers we interviewed, the many challenges strengthened their resilience.

Skaalvik and Skaalvik (2014) found that job-satisfaction, the perception of being competent in the job, and perceived autonomy correlated negatively with burnout and emotional exhaustion. Even though the stories tell about difficult situations, challenges with students and the praxis of teaching, 'our' teachers from five different countries met the problems with a positive attitude and determination to persist. In retrospect, critical reflections enabled them to view the difficulties as learning situations out of which they developed professionally. Harfitt (2015) concludes in her study of two novice teachers' narratives in Hong Kong, that their on-job experiences and personal stories shaped the teachers' professional identity. Gu and Day (2007) argue that professional identities interact with experiences teacher have in school and contribute to developing resilience as teachers. It is between the first and second year of teaching that professional development is strongest (Henry, Bastian, & Fortner, 2011), which seems to be the case with the teachers in this book as well. They critically reflect on the first year of teaching, and seem to enter the second year with a stronger feeling of self-efficacy. They know what it means to be a teacher and they have been strengthened by having handled difficult situations.

All of the teachers said they will continue teaching the next year, yet not all are sure they will stay in the classroom for the rest of their professional career. This issue is worth taking a closer look at. When we, the authors of this book graduated from teacher education, it was, more or less, expected of us, and we thought so ourselves, that we would be teachers for the rest of our professional life. Today we are teachers, but teachers of teachers and not teachers of children. We did not change the profession, but we changed our teaching contexts. Research in the last decade suggests interesting developments in the career plans of young people. Savickas (2012) suggests that young people today do not plan for long-term careers within the same profession. Today, educated young people look for multiple possibilities and are less concerned about mutual obligations to the same place of work. This aligns with a study by Roness and Smith (2010) who found that about 25% of Norwegian student teachers who engaged in a one year teacher education programme following they discipline degree, did not intend to work as teachers. The education would look good on the curricula vita when applying for jobs. Moreover, Watt and Richardson (2008) looked specifically at novice teachers' motivation for teaching, and they also found that more than a quarter of the 1651 Australian novice teachers were 'highly engaged switchers'. Watt and Richardson (2008) describe this group as highly educated and successful teachers who enjoy teaching, however, they do not plan to stay long in the profession, and are likely to seek new challenges outside teaching. The ten teachers we interviewed for this book all want to continue teaching a second year, however, we do not, and probably neither do they know if they will be teaching for the rest of their professional career. However, as for now, these teachers do not add to the worrying attrition rates after the first year of teaching.

11 Lessons Learned

In this last section of the current chapter and of the book, we would like to present some of the lessons we learned from listening to stories of ten novice teachers from five different countries, Australia, England, Finland, Israel, and Norway.

We learned that the experiences of novice teachers depend, to a large degree, on contextual differences. The five countries have different frameworks and regulations for education and schooling. There are national traditions and policies which automatically affect the experiences of the first year of teaching. Examples of this were the status of the profession, the support systems in the first year, and working within a standardized assessment context or not. However, we noticed that the contextual differences are largely related to the specific work place, the school in which the novice teachers work. Some schools immediately include the newly employed teachers in the collegium, whereas in other schools the new teachers felt it was difficult to feel included and accepted, and that there were few opportunities for collaboration. Perhaps, there is not much to be done by the local principal or teachers to impact the national frameworks, however, they can make a huge difference locally, in every school, by helping the newly employed colleagues to feel at home, to help them learn the local school culture and to become familiar with practical daily issues.

A second lesson we learned was that all the novice teachers expressed a need for support and mentoring during the first year, independently of the context. Some were happy with the support they received, others less, but nobody ignored the need for support. There are different ways of supporting novice teachers, and a combination of several forms for support are likely to be more successful than just focusing on one form, e.g. individual mentoring with an appointed mentor. The Finnish novices experience group mentoring and are happy with that, whereas the most common form for mentoring is individual mentoring, mentor and mentee. A conclusion to be drawn from the stories presented in this book is that perhaps a combination of group and individual mentoring might be a good solution. In a group with other novice teachers there are lots of opportunities for peer support and mutual learning, whereas individual mentoring allows for personal attention and support. As regards mentoring, we also learned that there often is a lot of rhetoric in the concept. We heard about teachers who had a mentor in name, but the person was not always available or had been given no time to support the novice colleague. Mentoring has to be taken seriously, and structured support systems have to be created at the macro level, however, it is at the practical implementation level that mentoring really can be of help to beginning teachers. An additional point is that teachers who feel that they are welcomed by the whole staff, included, and feel confident to ask everybody for help, tell about positive experiences in the first year. In other words, supporting novice teachers is the responsibility of the whole school in addition to support at the system level, mainly in form of resources.

We were surprised to learn that the novice teachers' motivation for teaching was similar across contexts. The teachers talked about altruistic and intrinsic motifs for choosing teaching, they care about children, the subject, and want to make an impact on the society. This is an important message to be addressed, not only by researchers, but more so, by policy makers. To maintain motivation for teaching and to stay in the profession, teachers need to feel they can enact their pedagogical and disciplinary beliefs and teach according to professional values. In an era of increased accountability and control, many teachers feel they are being told what to do, and they have to spend time on documentation instead of spending time with the children. One of the Norwegian teachers clearly said that if the external pressure on teachers increases, he is likely to leave the profession as he is not able to be the kind of teacher that he wants to be. Research tells us that his views are shared by many teachers, novice as well as more experienced teachers.

In relation to the above lesson learned, the teachers told about developing good relationships with students, and often the most difficult students, as a major contributor to their satisfaction with teaching and confidence booster. We learned that relationships in general, and especially with students, were highly valued by all the teachers across contexts. Some of the teachers talked about crisis with difficult students, and even though they asked for advice from more experienced teachers, they often trusted themselves and their own intuition in handling the situation. When this happened, they felt they really had chosen the right profession for them. None of the teachers in this book talked about satisfaction if they succeeded in teaching according to external goals or completed the required material. This does not mean that they did not teach as required, but doing so, did not give them the same professional satisfaction. A conclusion to draw from this is that teachers need to feel they have the possibility to be student-oriented and not only material oriented. This is an important message for us all who are interested in strengthening the quality of teaching, wherever we are.

We hope that by reading the book, the readers will draw their own conclusions about what lessons can be learned from the stories of the 10 novice teachers from five different countries. Above we have summarised our main lessons learned, but when reading and re-reading the book, we will probably regret that we did not mention more. Listening to the wonderful, optimistic and resilient teachers who kindly shared their stories with us has not only made us more knowledgeable about the first phase of a professional career of teaching, but has also made us wiser and more reflective in our work as teacher educators.

References

Aspfors, A., & Bondas, T. (2013). Caring about caring: newly qualified teachers' experiences of their relationships within the school community. *Teachers and Teaching: Theory and Practice, 19*(3), 243–259.

Aspfors, J., & Fransson, G. (2015). Research on mentor education for mentors of newly qualified teachers: A qualitative meta-synthesis. *Teaching and Teacher Education, 48*, 75–86.

Caspersen, J., & Raaen, F. D. (2014). Novice teachers and how they cope. *Teachers and Teaching: Theory and Practice, 20*(2), 189–211.

Dalin, P., & Kitson, K. (2004). *School development: Theories and strategies : An International handbook.* London: Bloomsbury Publishing PLC. Retrieved from http://ebookcentral.proquest.com/lib/agder/detail.action?docID=436357

Day, C. (2007). Committed for life? Variations in teachers' work, lives and effectiveness. *Journal of Educational Change, 9*, 243–260.

Department of Education, UK Government. (2013). *Teachers' standards. Guidance for school leaders, school staff and governing bodies.* Retrieved February 9, 2017, from http://www.gov.uk/government/publications

Dicke, T., Elling, J., Schmeck, A., & Leutner, D. (2015). Reducing reality shock: The effects of classroom management skills training on beginning teachers. *Teaching and Teacher Education, 48*, 1–12.

Flores, M. A. (2006).Being a novice teacher in two different settings: Struggles, continuities, and discontinuities. *Teachers College Record, 108*(10), 2021–2052.

Flores, M. A., & Day, C. (2006). Contexts which shape and reshape new teachers' identities: A multi-perspective study. *Teaching and Teacher Education, 22*(2), 219–232.

Fresko, B., & Alhija, F. N.-A. (2009). When intentions and reality clash: Inherent implementation difficulties of an induction program for new teachers. *Teaching and Teacher Education, 25*(2), 278–284.

Gu, Q., & Day, C. (2007). Teachers' resilience: A necessary condition for effectiveness. *Teaching and Teacher Education, 23*, 1302–1316. doi:10.1016/j.tate.2006.06.006

Hagger, H., & Wilkin, M. (Eds.). (1993). *Mentoring: Perspectives on school-based teacher education*. London: Kogan Page.

Harfitt, G. J. (2015). From attrition to retention: A narrative inquiry of why beginning teachers leave and then rejoin the profession. *Asia-Pacific Journal of Teacher Education, 43*(1), 22–35. http://dx.doi.org/10.1080/1359866X.2014.932333

Hargreaves, A., & Fullan, M. (2000). Mentoring in the new millennium. *Theory into Practice, 39*(1), 50–56.

Heikkinen, H. L. T., Jokinen, H., & Tynjälä, P. (2012). *Peer group mentoring for teacher development*. Hoboken, NJ: Taylor & Francis.

Henry, G. T., Bastian, K. C., & Kevin Fortner, C. (2011). Stayers and leavers: Early-career teacher effectiveness and attrition. *Educational Researcher, 40*(6), 271–280. https://doi.org/10.3102/0013189X11419042

Hermansen, H., Lorentzen, M., Mausethagen, S., & Zlatanovic, T. (2018). Hva kjennetegner forskning på lærerrollen under Kunnskapsløftet? En forskningskartlegging av studier av norske lærere, lærerstudenter og lærerutdannere. *Acta Didactica, 12*(1), 1–36.

Hobson, A. J., Ashby, P., Malderez, A., & Tomlinson, P. D. (2009). Mentoring beginning teachers. What we know and what we don't. *Teaching and Teacher Education, 25*(1), 207–216. https://doi.org/10.1016/j.tate.2008.09.001

Hobson, A. J., Malderez, A., Tracey, L., Homer, M., Mitchell, N., Biddulph, M., Giannakaki, M. S., Rose, A., Pell, R. G., Roper, T., Chambers, G. N., & Tomlinson, P. D. (2007). *Newly qualified teachers' experiences of their first year of teaching. Findings from phase III of the becoming a teacher project*. Retrieved September 26, 2008, from http://www.dfes.gov.uk/research/data/uploadfiles/DCSF-RR 008%20v2.pdf

Johnson, B., Down, B., Le Cornu, R., Peters, J., Sullivan, A., Pearce, J., & Hunter, J. (2014). Promoting early career teacher resilience: A framework for understanding and acting. *Teachers and Teaching: Theory and Practice, 20*(5), 530e546. http://dx.doi.org/10.1080/13540602.2014.937957

Kelchtermans, G., & Ballet, K. (2002). Micropolitical literacy: Reconstructing a neglected dimension in teacher development. *International Journal of Educational Research, 37*(8), 755–767.

Kemmis, S., Heikkinen, H., Fransson, G., Aspfors, J., & Edwards-Groves, C. (2014). Mentoring of new teachers as a contested practice: Supervision, support and collaborative self-development. *Teaching and Teacher Education, 43*, 154–164.

Kyriacou, C., & Kunc, R. (2007). Beginning teachers' expectations of teaching. *Teaching and Teacher Education, 23*(8), 1246–1257.

Lambson, D. (2010). Novice teachers learning through participation in a teacher study group. *Teaching and Teacher Education, 26*, 1660–1668.

Maynard, T., & Furlong, J. (1993). Learning to teach and models of mentoring. In D. Macintyre, H. Hagger, & M. Wilkin (Eds.), *Mentoring-perspectives on school-based teacher education*. London: Kogan Page.

Morgan, M., Ludlow, L., Kitching, K., O'Leary, M., & Clarke, A. (2010). What makes teachers tick? Sustaining events in new teachers' lives. *British Educational Research Journal, 36*(2), 191–208.

Nesje, K., Brandmo, C., & Berger, J. L. (2018). Motivation to become a teacher: A Norwegian validation of the factors influencing teaching choice scale. *Scandinavian Journal of Educational Research, 62*(6), 813–831. doi:10.1080/00313831.2017.1306804

Nias, J. (1996). Thinking about feeling: The emotions in teaching. *Cambridge Journal of Education, 26*(3), 293–306.

OECD. (2005). *Making teaching an attractive career choice: Pointers for policy development*. Retrieved December 15, 2018, from http://www.oecd.org/edu/school/45399482.pdf

Richardson, P., & Watt, H. (2016). Factors influencing teaching choice: Why do future teachers choose the career? In J. Loughran & M. Hamilton (Eds.), *International handbook of teacher education* (pp. 275–304). Singapore: Springer.

Roness, D., & Smith, K. (2010). Stability in motivation during teacher education. *Journal of Education for Teaching, 36*(2), 169–185.

Savickas, M. L. (2012). Life design: A paradigm for career intervention in the 21st century. *Journal of Counseling & Development, 90*(1), 13–19.

Schaefer, L., Long, J. K., & Clandinin, D. J. (2012). Questioning the research on early career teacher attrition and retention. *Alberta Journal of Educational Research, 58*(1), 106–121.

Schuck, S., & Russell, T. (2005). Self-study. Critical friendship, and the complexities of teacher education. *Studying Teacher Education, 1*(2), 107–121.

Skaalvik, E. M., & Skaalvik, S. (2014). Teacher self-efficacy and perceived autonomy: Relations with teacher engagement, job satisfaction, and emotional exhaustion. *Psychological Reports: Employment Psychology & Marketing, 114*(1), 68–77.

Smith, K., Ulvik, M., & Helleve, I. (2013). *Førstereisen* [The first journey]. Oslo: Gyldendal. [in Norwegian]

Stephens, P., Tønnessen, F. E., & Kyriacou, C. (2004). Teacher training and teacher education in England and Norway: A comparative study of policy goals. *Comparative Education, 40*(1), 109–130.

Tiplic, D., Brandmo, C., & Elstad, E. (2015). Antecedents of Norwegian beginning teachers' turnover intentions. *Cambridge Journal of Education, 45*(4), 451–474. doi:10.1080/0305764X.2014.987642

Ulvik, M., & Langørgen, K. (2012). What is there to learn from a new teacher? Newly qualified teachers as a resource in schools. *Teachers and Teaching: Theory and Practice, 18*(1), 43–57.

Ulvik, M., Smith, K., & Helleve, I. (2009). Novice in secondary school. The coin has two sides. *Teaching and Teacher Education, 25*(6), 835–842.

Watt, H. M. G., & Richardson, P. W. (2008). Motivations, perceptions, and aspirations concerning teaching as a career for different types of beginning teachers. *Learning and Instruction, 18*(5), 408–428. doi:10.1016/j.learninstruc.2008.06.002

Watt, H. M. G., Richardson, P. J., & Smith, K. (2017). Why teach? How teachers' motivations matter around the world. In H. Watt, P. Richardson, & K. Smith (Eds.), *Global perspectives on teacher motivation* (pp. 1–21). Cambridge: Cambridge University Press.